Searching for Sanity

52 Insights from Parents of the Bible

By

Lindsey Bell

Lighthouse Publishing
of the Carolinas
www.lighthousepublishingofthecarolinas.com

Foreword

Ever so often we are fortunate enough to meet someone who is eminently likeable, exceptionally talented and absolutely genuine. Lindsey Bell is such a woman, and I have been blessed to have her in my life.

Her delightful transparency and down-to-earth approach shine on every page of this lovely devotional. Lindsey guides us mothers on a journey of faith and motherhood.

Sharing out of her personal stock of experiences with heart-breaking miscarriages and the breathless anticipation (and plain old hard work!) of adoption, her authenticity, struggles and solutions line pages that you'll mark up, dog ear and return to again and again.

I invite you to pour your glass of Diet Coke, grab your mug of coffee (or both if it's been one of those days) and start your days with tender encouragement for moms. It will almost be like Lindsey is sitting there across from the table and swapping stories about the Crayon marks on her own!

Warmly,

Cindy Sigler Dagnan
Speaker & Author
www.cindydagnan.com

Praise for *Searching for Sanity...*

Parenting tips from actual parents in the Bible? Brilliant. Sincere and inspiring, Lindsey Bell gently nudges us to parent better by studying the lives of those who line the pages of the Bible. From the more well- known parents of the Bible (Mary) to the more obscure (Eunice), Bell highlights the lessons we can learn from each.

~ Amy Sullivan
Author

Lindsey and her husband, Keith, are a beautiful picture of what parenting really is. Through their pain, their trials, and their triumphs they have remained faithful to their family and to their God. The insights and encouragement you will receive in this book come from two of our greatest resources: the Word of God and real life experience. What more could you ask for?

~ Andy Turner
Minister of discipleship
Father of two

This weekly Bible Study format takes you through even the most unlikely parenting role models of the Bible. The journaling prompts, thought- provoking questions, and daily assignments will help focus you and keep your eyes on our Savior, Jesus Christ. A well- written and inspired book. A definite must read for any parent!

~ Annette Breedlove
Blogger at In All You Do
Mother of four earthly blessings

Lindsey opened my eyes to new biblical insights and made stories I've read dozens of times seem fresh. The weekly lessons are do~able, even for the busiest of mothers, yet full of meaning and practical application.

~ **Bekki Lindner**
Mother
Pastor's wife
Blogger at Chasing Supermom

Beginning on page one of the first devotion in *Searching for Sanity*, I wanted to hug Lindsey both to say, "I hear you, girl" and "Thank you!" This book packs in 52 weeks of Biblical parenting wisdom, relatable personal stories from Lindsey, and practical action steps even a busy mother of young children can begin to incorporate. Lindsey offers all this with understanding and a solid, yet gentle reminder to look to God, our Father, for whatever we need on this amazing, tiring, grace~ given journey of parenting.

~ **Caroline Flory**
Mother
Writer
Blogger at Under God's Mighty Hand

If sanity is on the short list of things you've recently misplaced, *Searching for Sanity* is your guidebook back to the main road. Using Biblical parents as models, Bell empathizes with your parenting world and includes insightful study questions and personal anecdotes in one great package.

~ **Cindy Sigler Dagnan**
Author
Speaker
Mother of four

Searching for Sanity is an excellent resource for parents everywhere. Using the Bible as our road map and following the examples of our Fathers and Mothers in the Lord, this tool will help equip even the most unqualified in their roles as godly parents.

~ Heather Knopp
Blogger at Raising Mighty Arrows

For many moms, there are two things that are hard to find: time with the Lord and peace in the midst of days that are often hectic. *Searching for Sanity* provides both. It helps moms take a breath, learn from the parents of the Bible, and walk away refreshed and ready for the day. Mothers of young children, you're in good hands! Read everything Lindsey writes!"

~ Jackina Stark
Author and Speaker

As a Children's Pastor, I wish every mom at our church would read this book. Bell does a great job of blending real life situations with God's timeless Word. Her reflection questions and activities each week really help apply God's Word to everyday life. This book helps you live out God's Word as you parent your children.

~ Jenny Fay
Children's Ministry Pastor at Canyon Ridge Christian Church, Las Vegas NV

Searching for Sanity offers encouraging insights for moms at all stages. Bell shows us how God used imperfect parents in the Bible to have an impact in the lives of their children and how He can use imperfect parents of today too. Short but provoking lessons, pointed questions, and practical every day applications make this book a must read for every busy mom.

~ Jody Hedlund
Bestselling Author
Busy Mother of five

Searching for Sanity proves the Bible is the perfect parenting tool. What better place to gain wisdom and be encouraged than by God himself. A must read for any parent!

~ Julie O'Connor
Mother of three

Lindsey's devotionals are short, sweet, and a perfect way for busy moms to start off their day. I loved the unique angle of studying and learning from parents of the Bible!

~ Katie Ganshert
Award~ winning author of *Wildflowers from Winter*

In *Searching for Sanity*, Bell has provided a valuable tool mothers can benefit from by reading alone or working through it with a group of other moms. Every reader will not only be encouraged to be her best, but will gain a deeper spiritual relationship with God. This book needs to be included in every baby shower gift as it is a must have for all young mothers.

~ Kimberly Wright
Author and Speaker
Mother of four

Lindsey's book is brilliant! *Searching For Sanity* is different than any other parenting book I've read. All parents wish there was a universal handbook we could follow to raise our kids. There is already one: the Bible. Lindsey uses the Bible in this book to learn from parents of old and point out relevant truths to modern parents. She asks pointed questions for reflection and journaling. And she lays out an activity each day to reinforce the weekly devotional. I wish I had read this book when I was expecting my oldest, so that I could have had a solid parenting plan in place. However, this book will help you develop a practical plan and structure for biblical parenting at any stage of parenthood. A must read.

~ Kristen Hamilton
Mother of three
Blogger at kristen~ hamilton.com
Contributor at Fancy Little Things

As a pastor, parent, and grandparent, it is exciting to find a book that is both biblical and helpful for families. Lindsey Bell has provided a masterpiece full of amazing insights in *Searching for Sanity*. Her devotions are practical, heart~ felt, and a must read for any busy parent who wants to grow.

~ Kurt Bubna
Pastor
Author of *Epic Grace ~ Chronicles of a Recovering Idiot*

Searching for Sanity is a sweet respite in a mom's sometimes-stressful life. This devotional offers practical suggestions, Scriptures moms need, and authentic encouragement. Be refreshed today and pick up a copy—and bless the next year of your parenting.

~ Mary DeMuth
Author of *You Can Raise Confident Kids*

Lindsey speaks right to a mother's heart and need. Her all- too- relatable experiences let moms know she understands their struggles. Then, she applies Scripture to those challenges in a practical way that offers grace- filled encouragement to follow God's leading for our families. Every mom will benefit from her perspective and wisdom.

~ Melinda Means
Mom
Author
Blogger at Mothering From Scratch

I love the book and Lindsey's approach to parenting. This is a fantastic book for new moms!

~ Merrie Hansen
Devotional writer

We all need help in raising children. Most of the time we need some sanity, and that's exactly what *Searching for Sanity* by Lindsey Bell is all about. It offers thoughtful, helpful, and Biblical advice and help in raising your children. Lindsey shares insights that help us take a deep breath and realize that with God, we've got this. Time will pass fast so enjoy this book and enjoy your children with great sanity.

~ Robin Sigars
Senior Minister at Carterville Christian Church
Father of seven

Thousands of moms with young children often voice their concern through our online community that they struggle to find time with God. *Searching for Sanity* is perfect for the mother who has limited time but longs to spend time in the Word. With reflection questions, prayers, and activities to do throughout the week, it's a fantastic resource and just what these weary mamas need!

~ Ruth Schwenk
Speaker
Writer
Creator of The Better Mom

Lindsey has an amazing gift of pulling nuggets of parenting wisdom out of Bible stories we often glance over ~ or assume we know far too well. Whether the story holds a warning or offers a habit we need to develop, she helps moms who are desperate, tired, and doubting themselves to know that you don't have to be perfect; you just have to lean on God!

~ Sheila Wray Gregoire
Blogger at To Love, Honor and Vacuum

One of the many challenges of being a busy mother is finding focused time to be in the Word of God and allowing that truth to sustain you throughout your day. Lindsey Bell tightly packages each devotion with truth, reflective content, and soul- searching questions. *Searching for Sanity* would be a great resource for a few moments of solitude with a cup of coffee at the kitchen table or for a coffee house discussion among friends.

~ Stacey Spikereit

Mother of four

Children's Minister at Carterville Christian Church

In her devotional, *Searching for Sanity: 52 Insights from the Parents of the Bible*, Lindsey Bell inspires moms through her fresh approach to biblical insight and practical parenting. With 52 devotions, mothers are given words of wisdom they can apply to their daily lives throughout the year. I am honored to recommend *Searching for Sanity: 52 Insights from the Parents of the Bible* to mothers with children of every age.

~ Stephanie Shott

Author

Speaker

Founder of The M.O.M. Initiative,

a ministry devoted to helping the body of Christ make

mentoring missional

SEARCHING FOR SANITY: 52 INSIGHTS FROM PARENTS OF
THE BIBLE BY LINDSEY BELL
Published by Lighthouse Publishing of the Carolinas
2333 Barton Oaks Dr., Raleigh, NC, 27614

ISBN 978-1-938499-75-3
Copyright © 2014 by Lindsey Bell
Cover design by The Killion Group, www.thekilliongroupinc.com
Interior design by Reality Info Systems, www.Realityinfo.com

Available in print from your local bookstore, online, or from the
publisher at: www.lighthousepublishingofthecarolinas.com

For more information on this book and the author visit:
www.lindseymbell.com or www.lindsey-bell.com.

Scripture quotations are taken from the HOLY BIBLE NEW
INTERNATIONAL VERSION® NIV® Copyright© 1973, 1978,
1984 by International Bible Society. Used by permission of Zondervan
Publishing House. All rights reserved.

Brought to you by the creative team at
LighthousePublishingoftheCarolinas.com:
Amberlyn Edwards, Eddie Jones, Meaghan Burnett, Rowena Kuo, and
Brian Cross.

Library of Congress Cataloging-in-Publication Data
Bell, Lindsey.
Searching for Sanity: 52 Insights from Parents of the Bible / Lindsey
Bell 1st ed.

Printed in the United States of America

Contents

Acknowledgements

To my husband, Keith. Thank you for believing in me when I doubted myself. When my first article was published, you framed it for me and have shared in my excitement ever since. Thank you for giving me time to write and edit. Thank you for never grumbling because I didn't do something else during naptime. Years ago, you told me I didn't know how to fail, and those words have encouraged me many times.

To my boys, Rylan and Caden. Rylan, I will never forget the day your daddy and I found out you were going to join our family. I was awestruck. You are my love and my joy. I am so thankful to God for you, my firstborn son and my miracle baby. And Caden, I believe with all of my heart you are God's gift to me. You are an answer to prayer and part of God's plan to heal my heart and make our family complete. I am forever grateful to your birthparents who chose to give us such a wonderful gift. I adore you and am blessed by you daily.

To my parents, Chuck and Eve Poznich, who taught me what it means to sacrifice your desires for those you love. You gave me so much more than I deserve and left me an amazing example to follow. I hope someday my kids look up to me as much as I look up to you.

To my family: my brothers Jason and Jared, my nieces and nephews, my in-laws, all of our grandparents, and our extended families. Thank you for loving me even when I wasn't easy to love. Thank you for asking about this book and showing an interest in what I do.

To my agent, Blythe Daniel. Thank you for taking a chance on a young writer like me. Your support pushed me to be a better writer. You challenged me to do things that were beyond my comfort level, and I am grateful for your advice, expertise, and encouragement.

To my stellar team at Lighthouse Publishing of the Carolinas: Amberlyn, Eddie, Meaghan, and Rowena. Amberlyn, thank you for patiently guiding me to make this book the best it could be and for bearing with me as I'm sure I made all sorts of newbie mistakes. Your patient guidance and wisdom have been invaluable to me.

To my friends who read the very first draft (unpolished and full of annoying mistakes, I'm sure): Mandy Young, Julie O'Connor, Keri Jane Churchill, and Kim Kirschner. Thank you for being honest with me and offering great advice.

To the amazing group of moms and others at Carterville Christian Church who believed in me and in the message of this book and to those at my home church (First Christian Church in Miami) who never stopped cheering me on.

To LeAnn Campbell who went above and beyond as a writing mentor. You were the first one to read and edit this devotional, and your advice was invaluable.

To my writer friends who helped me along the way: those of you with CWF and those of you with HACWN. I owe so much to both of these groups. You helped me with edits and tips, gave me tons of advice, and even opened the door for me to find my agent.

To teachers who believed in me and encouraged my writing as I grew up: Mrs. Levo, Mrs. Oexman, Mrs.

Stephens, and Jackina Stark. Mrs. Stephens, when you allowed us to turn in the same assignment over and over again until we got it right, you taught me to edit and helped me learn how to make my writing shine. And Jackina, your assignment to send in an article is what began my journey along this path of writing. I owe so much to these and other phenomenal teachers along the way.

To Cindy Dagnan for encouraging me in this writing journey and for supporting this book. I am honored to have your support.

Finally—and most importantly—to God for enabling me to write. It is your grace that enables me to write and your Word that gives me something to write about. This book is my offering to you. I pray you make it a blessing to those who read it.

Dedication

For Rylan and Caden, my car-loving boys who make me laugh and know exactly how to melt my mommy-heart. Without you, I would have no book to write.

Week 1:
The Search Begins

Your word, LORD, is eternal; it stands firm in the heavens.[1] Psalm 119:89

As my husband drove us home from the hospital with our newborn baby sleeping in the backseat, I began to cry. *What have I gotten myself into? I'm not ready to be a mom. I have no idea what I'm doing.*

The excitement of expecting a child wore off as reality set in. This tiny baby was now ours to care for, teach, and raise into a man of God. We weren't even home from the hospital, and I was already overwhelmed with my new responsibilities.

If only there were a handbook or a guide to parenthood. I wanted steps that guaranteed success. Unfortunately, there isn't a handbook. As I struggled in my new role as a mom, I searched the Internet, read books and magazines, and consulted other parents for advice. The information from these sources was valuable, but it never completely satisfied my heart.

It was only when I turned to God's Word that I found what I was looking for. God may not have given us a handbook, but He certainly didn't leave us empty-handed.

The psalmist says God's Word is eternal. Because of its eternal nature, we can rest assured that even if everything else fails, God's Word won't. It might not answer every question we ask or provide us step-by-step instruction, but it will help us nonetheless. We can turn to it on those days when we feel lost or wonder what we should do next.

In the days ahead, we will explore both the good and bad parents of the Bible. What did they do well? What did they do poorly? We'll study their lives and seek to learn from the One who invented parenthood.

One theme you'll see throughout is that none of the parents in the Bible were perfect. (I, for one, am thankful for that.) They were just like you and me: trying to do their best, while at the same time wondering if they did anything right. They made mistakes, and their children made mistakes—sometimes tragic ones that changed the entire direction of their lives. But God still used them. He'll use us too. Assuming, of course, we are willing to ask.

Questions for Reflection:

1. How did you feel when you became a parent? Journal your thoughts.

2. Where do you look for parenting advice? From whom do you seek wisdom?

3. What is the best piece of advice you have ever received?

4. What is the worst piece of advice?

5. When you think of parents of the Bible, who first comes to your mind? Eve, the very first mother? Or Sarah? Maybe Hannah? Or Mary, the mother of Jesus?

Prayer:

Father in heaven, you are the One who invented parenthood. Guide me in the days to come as I seek to learn from you. Provide me with insights that are applicable to my family. Help me to learn exactly what you want me to learn. Amen.

Activities:

Day 1 – Starting this week, journal your thoughts as you go through this devotional. What are you learning? How is God speaking to you? Continue to journal each week as you read.

Day 2 – Choose one or two other mothers who are willing to meet with you on a weekly basis. Use these opportunities to pray together and discuss parenting strategies.

Day 3 – Start praying with your children every night before they go to bed. If they are old enough to talk, ask them to pray too. Try to continue this habit even after you finish this devotional.

Day 4 – In your journal, write one quality you want to improve upon over the next year. Maybe you want to develop a fruit of the Spirit like love, joy, peace, or patience. Or maybe you want to become a better steward of your time or talents.

Day 5 – Ask an older woman whom you admire to pray for you throughout the year.

WEEK 2:
EVE

Adam made love to his wife Eve, and she became pregnant and gave birth to Cain. She said, "With the help of the LORD I have brought forth a man." Genesis 4:1

Eve isn't typically known for her great mothering abilities. Instead, when people think of her, they often recall that she was the first woman God created or the one who brought sin into the world. They might remember how one of her children, Cain, killed another one of her children. But they are probably not thinking they want to be just like her. You might wonder, then, why I'm beginning this devotional with her story.

I'm beginning with Eve because she did one crucial thing right. When her children were born, she remembered to thank the Lord before she did anything else. With Cain, her firstborn, she said, *"With the help of the LORD I have brought forth a man"* (Genesis 4:1). Then, after giving birth to Seth, she said, *"God has granted me another child in place of Abel, since Cain killed him"* (Genesis 4:25).

I don't know about you, but I didn't even think about God right after delivery. I thought about the intense pain, about my new baby boy, and about getting everything "down there" covered up. There was too much going on to remember to thank God.

Or maybe that was just my excuse. Because if I had really wanted to focus on Him, I would have. When I want to focus on a television show or on my computer, I can manage to do that. The problem is that I don't really want to focus on God all the time.

When my oldest son, Rylan, was two years old, he developed a method for focusing. When he didn't want to hear something, he covered his ears. As a mother who wanted her child to listen to her every word, it was frustrating. But I have to admit, it was also smart. By blocking out everything around him, he was able to focus on what he wanted.

Eve also was able to block out the distractions around her so she could focus on the Lord and on what He had done for her. She made a lot of mistakes in her lifetime, but *this* she did right. *This* is worth emulating.

Questions for Reflection:

1. What is most difficult about focusing on God in your everyday life?

2. Who or what tends to slip into the number one spot in your life? Why?

3. What helps keep your mind on God throughout the day?

Prayer:

Lord, I desire to focus on you throughout each day. Forgive me for times when I allow other people or things to slip into your designated spot in my mind and heart. Help me to keep you as my number one priority, above everything and everyone else. Amen.

Activities:

Day 1 – Develop a daily devotion time. What time of the day would best fit your personality and schedule? Are mornings or evenings typically better? Make an effort to spend time with the Lord every single day. (But remember, Mom, to cut yourself some slack. God is not going to punish you if you miss a day or two ... or even several days.)

Day 2 – Watch for teachable moments and opportunities to teach your kids through everyday life. Try to find at least one teachable moment today.

Day 3 – Every night at dinnertime this week, ask your children how they have seen the Lord. Did they see Him in the beautiful sunrise, or in the kind actions of a friend? Did they see Him in their Bible-reading time? If your children aren't yet talking, tell them how you have seen God working in your life.

Day 4 – Begin worshiping daily. Whether to a children's

Bible song CD or to worship tunes on your computer, sing to the Lord every day. You can choose to sing with your kids or do it in private.

Day 5 – Spend fifteen minutes outside, admiring God's creation and listening for His voice.

WEEK 3:
NOAH AND KORAH

This is the account of Noah and his family. Noah was a righteous man, blameless among the people of his time, and he walked faithfully with God. Noah had three sons: Shem, Ham and Japheth. Genesis 6:9-10

and the earth opened its mouth and swallowed them and their households, and all those associated with Korah, together with their possessions. Numbers 16:32

My oldest son loves the movie *Cars,* and truth be told, I enjoy it too. There's only one drawback to the movie: a few words that aren't exactly appropriate for a preschooler. One such example is Mater (if you're not familiar with the movie, Mater is the old, beat-up tow truck—hilarious and a little rough around the edges), who likes the phrase, "Holy shoot." Not bad words, but also not something I want my son repeating to his Sunday school teacher.

After all, children love to copy. We can count on them to repeat everything they hear, even those less-than-desirable words we accidentally let slip from our mouths. They especially love to copy their parents. Why wouldn't they? We are their heroes. We are the ones who teach them what to say, how to react, and what to do. Whether we like it or not, our actions as parents affect our children. This could not be more evident than in the lives of biblical figures, Noah and Korah.

You're probably familiar with Noah. When God sent a flood to destroy the world, He saved Noah and his family. This story is found in Genesis 6-9. The account begins by describing how wicked the world had become. In the midst of this wickedness, though, God noticed Noah's righteousness. The Bible doesn't talk about the righteousness of Noah's sons: Shem, Ham and Japheth. It only talks about the righteousness of Noah. It was Noah's behavior that saved his family and his holiness that protected them from the waters. Noah's story is the polar opposite of Korah's.

Korah, unlike Noah, led his family to destruction. He's one of those biblical characters we don't typically read about. His story, found in Numbers 16, is one we tend to skip when choosing a bedtime story for our children. Here's a summary of what happened: God chose Moses as the leader of the Israelite people—out of slavery in Egypt, through the desert, and toward the Promised Land. While journeying through the desert, Korah rebelled against Moses and led

250 others to question Moses' authority. As punishment for his rebellion, God caused the earth to swallow Korah and his entire household (children included).

What a difference between Noah and Korah. Noah's righteousness led to the salvation of his family, while Korah's wickedness led to the destruction of his. Fifty years after I'm gone, I wonder what people will say about me: that I led my family to salvation, or that I led them to destruction.

What do you think people will say about you?

Questions for Reflection:

1. Describe a time when your children mirrored positive behavior.

2. Describe a time when your children copied negative behavior.

3. In what ways have you followed in the footsteps of your parents?

4. When your children are grown, what is one character trait you want them to display?

5. What can you do now to help build that trait in them?

Prayer:

Father in heaven, make me like Noah, whose righteousness led to his family's salvation. Help me remember that my actions affect not just myself, but also my family. When I'm tempted to sin, remind me that my sins can hurt my family too. Amen.

Activities:

Day 1 – Play a game of Follow the Leader with your
         children.

Day 2 – Count how many times your child tries to copy
         your behavior or follow your lead today.

Day 3 – Write in your journal any words you want to cut
         from your vocabulary.

Day 4 – Identify thoughts you want to eliminate from
         your mind. Write them in your journal as you
         think of them.

Day 5 – Carry a small mirror with you as a reminder that
         your kids mirror your behavior.

WEEK 4: HAGAR

God heard the boy crying, and the angel of God called to Hagar from heaven and said to her, "What is the matter, Hagar? Do not be afraid; God has heard the boy crying as he lies there." Genesis 21:17

I failed my child. At least, that's what I thought at the time. When my son Rylan was a newborn, we tried to breastfeed for eight weeks with no success. Then, at nine weeks, he began losing weight. I had assumed breastfeeding would come naturally. But for us, it didn't. Never before had I felt like such a failure. I let my child down, and I let myself down.

Have you been there? You want so much to be a good mother but can't help feeling like a failure. Regardless of whether or not your feelings are justified, you can't get the nagging thoughts out of your mind. Thoughts like these:

You're not a good mom.

Look at how she does it. It's so easy for her.

You must be doing something wrong to have a child who behaves this way.

Look at this house. A good mom wouldn't let it get this messy.

The lies might look different to every mother, but the source is the same. Satan wants us to believe we are failures. He wants us to believe someone else could do it better and that we're not worth anything.

God, on the other hand, wants to tell us something completely different. He wants to show us salvation. He wants to take us by the hand and give us hope when we feel defeated and alone, just like He did with Hagar.

Hagar was Abraham and Sarah's slave and the mother of Abraham's son Ishmael. After Sarah delivered Isaac, she wanted nothing to do with Hagar and Ishmael. She didn't want them to interfere with her son's life, so she sent them into the desert to fend for themselves. A few days later, when their food and water were gone, Hagar lost all hope. Her son was dying of thirst in the desert, and she couldn't bear to watch him, so she left him alone to die. In her brokenness, the Lord opened her eyes to their salvation: a well of water.

This is not the only instance in the Bible when God opened someone's eyes and enabled them to see something they needed to see. In 2 Kings 6, enemy armies surrounded the prophet Elisha and his servant. Take a look at this text: *When the servant of the man of God got up and went out early the next morning, an army with horses and chariots had surrounded the city. "Oh no, my lord! What shall we do?" the servant asked. "Don't be afraid," the prophet answered. "Those who are with us are more than those who are with them." And Elisha prayed, "Open his eyes, LORD, so that he may see." Then the LORD opened the servant's eyes, and he looked and saw the hills full of horses and chariots of fire all around Elisha* (2 Kings 6:15-17).

Elisha's servant didn't need to win the war. He didn't need the Lord to remove his struggle. All he needed was to see His salvation.

Sometimes that's all we need too. We need to see that there's hope, that things will improve, and that we are doing a good job. When we feel like we can't go on anymore, we need God to open our eyes to His hope.

And let me reassure you, dear mother. He will give you hope when there's no hope to be found. He gave it to me when I needed it, and He will give it to you too.

Questions for Reflection:

1. Describe a time in which you felt defeated as a parent. How did you get through this difficult time?

2. What is one area of your life in which you are currently struggling?

Prayer:

Lord, open my eyes to see how you are working in my life and in the lives of my children. Help me see my problems as you see them. When life is difficult, allow me to remain hopeful. Amen.

Activities:

Day 1 – Write a letter of encouragement to someone who is struggling. Ask your children to help. If they aren't yet old enough to write, allow them to color the card you write.

Day 2 – Take a look at Acts 7, and read about another biblical figure whose eyes God opened. (Pay special attention to the end of the chapter.)

Day 3 – Do something for yourself. Take a bath, go for a run, or get a pedicure.

Day 4 – Make a list of five things for which you are thankful.

Day 5 – If you are married, do something for your spouse to encourage his parenting efforts.

Week 5:
Abraham

"Do not lay a hand on the boy," he said. "Do not do anything to him. Now I know that you fear God, because you have not withheld from me your son, your only son." Genesis 22:12

I've made a few minor sacrifices in my lifetime. I've given my last piece of candy to my husband because he didn't have any left. I've eaten at restaurants I don't like because someone else wanted to eat there. I've occasionally lost sleep to help someone in need. But that's about it. For the most part, I'm clueless about what it means to sacrifice. Abraham, on the other hand, understood sacrifice well.

In Genesis 22, God told Abraham to sacrifice his son as a burnt offering. Imagine Abraham's confusion. First, God promised Abraham he would be the father of many nations (See Genesis 17). Then God told him to kill his only son. It wasn't like he and Sarah had other kids to carry on his family line. Isaac was it. If Isaac died, there was no back-up plan. How was he supposed to father many nations without any children?

Abraham faced the most difficult decision of his life: his son or his God? From the looks of it, Abraham didn't even hesitate. When God told Abraham to sacrifice Isaac as a burnt offering, Abraham woke up *early the next morning* and prepared to murder his son (Genesis 22:3). Abraham had never heard Jesus' warning in Matthew 10:37—*Anyone who loves their son or daughter more than me is not worthy of me*—but if he had, he would have been the first to obey. His God was more important than his children. Period.

I wish I could say the same. But in reality, my God doesn't always come first. I don't want to wake up early to spend time with Him, so I choose sleep. I don't want to sacrifice my desires for my husband's, so I choose myself. I don't want to put God above my children, so I choose my sons.

It's not a conscious decision, of course, to put myself and others before God. It just happens, little by little. My thoughts, rather than focusing on the Lord, focus on my kids. My time, rather than spending it for God, is spent on my own agenda. I live life for myself and for my family.

What God is asking of me, though, is to live life for Him, first and foremost. To sacrifice my dreams, my plans, and my agenda—for Him. God is asking me to think about Him more than I think about my children and to live for Him rather than to live for myself.

God chose me—above His one and only child. All He's asking is for me to return the favor.

Questions for Reflection:

1. What practical steps can you take to keep God at the center of your life?

2. How would you react if God asked you to sacrifice your child? Journal your thoughts.

3. Why is it difficult to love God more than our children?

Prayer:

Father, thank you for choosing me even though I don't deserve it. Help me to choose you—above my spouse, above my children, and above every other relationship. You, Lord, most certainly deserve all of my adoration. Amen.

Activities:

Day 1 – Take thirty minutes to be alone with God. He gave His son; surely we can give a half hour.

Day 2 – Practice the art of sacrifice by giving up something you want for your child. Maybe it's a nap or thirty minutes to yourself. Give it up to spend time with your child.

Day 3 – Practice the art of sacrifice by giving up something you desire for your spouse. Maybe it's a favorite candy bar you've been hiding from the rest of the family that you will now share. Or maybe it's a night away—a night that you wanted but are now giving to him.

Day 4 – Teach your children about sacrifice by asking them to choose a toy to give to a family in need.

Day 5 – Give up something you enjoy for at least 24 hours, if not longer (examples: the Internet, television, your cell phone, Facebook, Pinterest, coffee, or candy).

WEEK 6:
REBEKAH

*Isaac, who had a taste for wild game, loved
Esau, but Rebekah loved Jacob.* Genesis 25:28

It was my twentieth birthday and two weeks before my wedding when I first learned life is not fair. Another driver veered into my lane of traffic, sent me into a ditch, and totaled my car. My "life-is-fair" mindset assured me she would get a ticket, pay for damages, and learn to be a more cautious driver. She didn't, because life isn't always fair. We don't always get what we deserve.

I learned the lesson again recently. My husband and I have two boys: one biological and one adopted. We want another biological child and have been trying for years. Unfortunately, instead of another baby, we have endured multiple miscarriages. Four miscarriages in three years to be exact.

If life were fair, everyone who wanted a baby would have one.

If life were fair, bad things wouldn't happen to good people.

But life isn't fair. It's a lesson we all struggle to learn at one time or another.

I bet our biblical figure for the day struggled with this lesson too. After all, when Jacob was growing up, his mother did everything in her power to make sure life was fair for him—even when it meant deceiving his father and stealing from his brother.

When I first read this story, I thought to myself, *what kind of mother would do that? What kind of mother would encourage her son to pretend to be someone else, even disguise himself, just to get a blessing?* But then I saw myself in Rebekah's story. Rebekah only wanted what was best for her son. She didn't want his father to treat him unfairly, because she believed he deserved better.

Every mother wants the best for her children. When a teacher doesn't give them the grade they deserve, when someone makes fun of them, or when a group of friends leaves them out of their weekend plans ... we want more for them. We don't want to see our children hurting, so we step in and do everything in our power to prevent any pain from entering their lives. Even if it means teaching our kids that it's okay to bend the rules.

We want life to be fair for them, but it's not. The earlier our children learn this lesson, the better they will adapt to life's struggles. Instead of seeking what they think they deserve, they will learn to accept whatever God allows into their lives.

There's one person in the Bible who did just that. His name was Jesus. When He stood before Pilate, He could have challenged the religious leaders and pleaded for justice. They were, after all, condemning Him on false charges. But Jesus didn't challenge their decision. He didn't seek His rights. He didn't fight for what He deserved. His goal was not for life to be fair, but for us to be free.

I, for one, am thankful Jesus valued our freedom so much.

Questions for Reflection:

1. Describe a time in which you have stepped in to make certain your child received what he/she deserved. What was the end result?

2. Why is it difficult to watch people treat your children unfairly?

3. When has someone treated you unfairly? What did you learn through this experience?

Prayer:

Lord, thank you that life isn't fair. I know I want it to be fair sometimes. But help me remember that if it were, Jesus never would have died on the cross to make me whole. Forgive me when I forget this important truth. Amen.

Activities:

Day 1 – Read Matthew 20:1-15. What does this parable teach us about God's fairness?

Day 2 – Create an opportunity to teach your children life is not fair. Try to allow each of your children the experience of being on the losing end and winning end of your generosity. (For instance, you could purchase one large candy bar and one small one. Or you could give one child more time with a certain toy.)

Day 3 – List five reasons you are thankful life is not fair.

Day 4 – Give someone your place in line today.

Day 5 – Look up the story of Joseph in your Bible. (His story begins in Genesis 37 and runs through Genesis 50. Pay special attention to Genesis 50:19-21. How did Joseph react when life wasn't fair?)

WEEK 7:
ISAAC AND REBEKAH

So Isaac called for Jacob and blessed him.
Then he commanded him: "Do not marry a
Canaanite woman." Genesis 28:1

Kari's[2] dad wasn't around, so she looked to other men for the love he never gave. She didn't go to church and didn't have a relationship with God. Then she met Josh, who invited her to church. Now, they are married and serve in ministry together. Kari told me recently, "Josh invited me to church sixteen years ago, and my life has never been the same." As Kari learned, few people can influence us like our spouses.

Isaac and Rebekah seem to have known this because when Jacob was ready to marry, they sent him away from their Canaanite neighbors to find a woman who would share his faith in God. Unfortunately, they didn't do the same with Esau, their other son. For some reason, they didn't think to offer him this same advice.

I feel bad for the guy, don't you? First, Jacob steals his

blessing. Then, Jacob receives the advice no one thought to give Esau. The Bible isn't clear on why Isaac and Rebekah only focused on Jacob's wife and not Esau's. Maybe it was because Jacob was the one God promised to bless. Or maybe it was because Rebekah needed some excuse to get Jacob out of town, away from his angry brother.

Or maybe (and I think most likely), they learned from their mistake with Esau. They didn't say anything about Esau's wives, and he married several Canaanite women—women who could easily lead him away from the Lord. They didn't want the same for Jacob. With him, they wouldn't take any chances. With him, they would do whatever they could to find a godly spouse.

We would be wise to follow suit. Our children's spouses will either draw them to God or push them away. A part of me wants to think I will always be the most important woman in my sons' lives. But I know I won't. When my boys marry, their wives will become the most important people on earth to them. More important than me. More important than their daddy. More important than their friends. This is all the more reason to start praying for their future wives now, before it's too late.

Questions for Reflection:

1. Whom have you dated? How did each of these people affect you?

2. At what age do you want to allow your children to begin dating?

3. If you are married, how has your spouse affected you? (Both positively and negatively.)

4. What other steps can you take to prepare your children for marriage?

Prayer:

Father, you designed marriage to be a testimony of your love—an example of what real love looks like. Strengthen my marriage so it fulfills that purpose. Guide my children to spouses who will draw them closer to you. Amen.

Activities:

Day 1 – If you are married, go on a date with your spouse.

Day 2 – If you are married, tell your husband how he has affected your life and ask how you have affected his.

Day 3 – If you aren't married, make a list of the qualities you want in a mate.

Day 4 – Talk with someone (your husband if you're married) about when you want to allow your children to date. Seek the wisdom of other parents as well.

Day 5 – Talk with another couple about rotating date nights. (You watch their kids for their date. Then they watch your kids for your date.)

WEEK 8:
JACOB

Now Israel [also known as Jacob] loved Joseph more than any of his other sons, because he had been born to him in his old age; and he made an ornate robe for him.
Genesis 37:3 (note added)

When my son Rylan was about two-and-a-half, I scheduled a play date with a friend of mine. Call it naivety or stupidity, but I thought Rylan would play well with my friend's younger child. I envisioned them playing together, sharing and giggling the entire time. Unfortunately, this is not at all what happened. The first toy my friend's son held, Rylan grabbed. Then the hitting began. Who knew my son was so possessive? He refused to share any of his toys with this poor child.

Joseph's brothers certainly experienced this type of jealousy (but in a more extreme way). Their father Jacob (known as Israel in this text) had twelve sons, born from several mothers. Rather than love each of his sons equally, he favored Joseph, one of the sons born to his favorite wife, Rachel. Sibling rivalry resulted, and Joseph's brothers eventually sold Joseph into slavery.

We likely won't have to worry about one child selling another into slavery, but all of us will face sibling rivalry or jealousy of some kind. Even if we have only one child, this child will—at some point or another—fight with someone over something. Our youngest son is not even two yet, and we have already begun to face this issue. "It's my toy ... Give it back ... I want to sit on your lap, Mommy ... He took my car." The sibling wars start early, and unfortunately, we can't totally prevent them.

Our first-born will try to protect his turf. Our later-born might try to do whatever necessary to make a name for himself. Our middle child might feel overlooked. Our earlier-born might resent the special privileges the youngest seems to receive. We can't prevent the rivalry, but there is one thing we can do. We can make sure our behavior doesn't make it worse.

I've often wondered what would have happened if Israel had loved each of his sons equally. Maybe the brothers wouldn't have sold Joseph. Maybe Israel wouldn't have lived most of his adult life mourning a son he thought was dead. One bad decision—giving one son a special gift while neglecting the rest—changed his life. At least we can learn from his story and treat each of our children with the love they so desperately need.

Questions for Reflection:

1. Which of your children do you connect with most naturally? Why?

2. With which of your children do you have the most difficult time connecting? Why?

3. What is one thing you can do with your difficult child this week to strengthen your bond?

Prayer:

Lord, thank you for each of my children. Thank you for not making them identical, but instead giving them unique gifts and personalities. Help me love each of them equally. On those days when one child is more difficult, remind me of your love. Guide me to love them as you love me. Amen.

Activities:

Day 1 – Spend individual time with each of your children today. Go on a Mommy/Child date.

Day 2 – Determine the love languages of each of your children. For more information, check out *The Five Love Languages of Children* by Gary Chapman and Ross Campbell (Northfield Publishing: Chicago, 1997).

Day 3 – Evaluate how your parents treated you. Did you feel as though they loved you and your siblings equally? Why or why not? Journal your thoughts.

Day 4 – Ask your kids about their favorite foods, activities, colors, etc.

Day 5 – Check out *The Birth Order Book: Why You Are the Way You Are* by Dr. Kevin Leman (Fleming H Revell: Grand Rapids, 1998). This book will help you understand not only yourself but also your children.

Week 9:
Jochebed

But when she could hide him no longer, she got a papyrus basket for him and coated it with tar and pitch. Then she placed the child in it and put it among the reeds along the bank of the Nile. Exodus 2:3

Jochebed laid the basket in the reeds along the river and walked away, unable to shake the nagging question in her mind: *could she trust God to take care of her little boy?* Imagine how difficult that must have been. Pharaoh had given the order that every Hebrew boy must be thrown into the Nile (Exodus 1:22). Jochebed had hidden her baby for three months. As he grew older, though, she was no longer able to keep him quiet. She knew she had to act before someone found him, so she got a basket and placed him inside. She put the basket among the reeds of the Nile River and waited. *Would God come through for her? Would He protect her child?*

At some point in our parenting journeys, all of us will likely ask a question similar to Jochebed's. I asked it before my son Rylan was born. At 21 weeks of pregnancy, I began having contractions. My doctor informed us that if he wasn't able to stop the contractions, he probably couldn't save our baby. *Could I trust God with this?* When our children's safety is out of our hands, will God take care of them?

Part of being a parent is learning to trust God. We can't be there for our children all the time, nor should we be. But, like Jochebed who trusted God enough to leave her baby in a basket in a river, we can trust Him to watch over our children.

I wish this meant He would prevent bad things from happening—no car wrecks, no sicknesses, no pain. I wish it meant they would live long, happy, pain-free lives. Unfortunately, it doesn't. Sometimes, God allows these things to happen to them. We may never understand why, but we can know this: He will work everything out for good. As Romans 8:28 promises, *We know that in all things God works for the good of those who love him, who have been called according to his purpose.*

Questions for Reflection:

1. What negative circumstances have you gone through in your life?

2. How has God used these circumstances for good?

3. Why does God allow bad things to happen to His people?

4. When have you struggled to trust God?

5. If you had been Jochebed, what would you have done with Moses?

Prayer:

God, sometimes I wonder why you don't stop bad things from happening to me and to those I love. Build my faith, and use any negative circumstances for good. I know you are able, and I choose to trust you with my future and with the futures of my children. Amen.

Activities:

Day 1 – Memorize Romans 8:28 with your children.

Day 2 – Read about Christians who are being persecuted at the Voice of the Martyrs' website: http://www.persecution.com/.

Day 3 – List every negative circumstance you've ever experienced. Pray over the list. Then destroy it as a reminder that God is bigger than every problem you face.

Day 4 – Make a basket out of Play-doh with your children. Tell them the story of baby Moses.

Day 5 – Help your kids reenact the story of Moses with a baby doll, basket, etc.

WEEK 10: ISRAELITES

These commandments that I give you today are to be on your hearts. Impress them on your children. Talk about them when you sit at home and when you walk along the road, when you lie down and when you get up. Tie them as symbols on your hands and bind them on your foreheads. Write them on the doorframes of your houses and on your gates. Deuteronomy 6:6-9

My journal is full of good intentions and things I want to improve upon. Unfortunately, many of these ideas never leave the pages of my journal. These good intentions—to read my Bible every day, have family devotions, exercise more, or whatever—seldom become reality. Somewhere along the way, probably between seven loads of laundry and the third temper tantrum of the morning, I forget about them.

Maybe that's why Moses made such a big deal about remembering God's commands. He knew our tendency to forget. In Deuteronomy 6:6-9, he gave the Israelites three strategies to help them remember.

First, he encouraged them to talk about God. He challenged the people to talk about God all day long, not just at bedtime or during devotion time. That means we should talk about Him throughout the day—when we're struggling with a defiant and angry two-year-old, when we're changing the fifth diaper of the day, and when we're coloring with our kindergartner. We have hundreds of opportunities to talk about God every day, but we must watch for these teachable moments. Otherwise, we'll likely miss them.

Second, Moses challenged them to carry the Word with them. I must admit, the thought of carrying another thing, especially a heavy book, disheartens me. My arms are already full, and my bags overflowing. But carrying the Word doesn't mean we have to carry the entire Bible. We can write our favorite verses on index cards, memorize key verses, or download a Bible on our phone, iPad or laptop. In today's world where technology is at our fingertips, there is no reason for any of us not to follow through with this one.

A third strategy Moses gave the Israelites was to display verses throughout their homes. At first glance, this seems easy. Write a verse on a card and stick it to a mirror, no problem. But just displaying the verse isn't enough. We have to actually stop what we're doing, take in our surroundings, and read the verses.

I think if I followed Moses' advice more often, those

journal entries would leave the pages and become reality. Those good intentions would become habits instead of things that might have been.

Questions for Reflection:

1. What spiritual habits would you like to develop with your family?

2. What steps can you take today to begin forming these habits?

3. Which of the three strategies seems most difficult for you? Why?

4. What teachable moments have you experienced in your household? Did you take advantage of these opportunities? Why or why not?

Prayer:

Lord, help me keep your Word in my mind. By it, I can fight temptation and know your will. By it, you will encourage and strengthen my faith. Use it to transform both my family and me. Amen.

Activities:

Day 1 – Choose one of the strategies to begin implementing today.

Day 2 – Write five verses on index cards to keep in your purse or car.

Day 3 – Write your children's favorite verses on construction paper. Display them in your home.

Day 4 – In your journal, record how you talked about
God throughout the day.

Day 5 – Start memorizing one verse a week or one verse a
month. Consider including your entire family in
this activity. (In Appendix B, you'll find 25 great
Bible verses to memorize with your family.)

WEEK 11:
ACHAN

*Then Joshua, together with all Israel, took
Achan son of Zerah, the silver, the robe, the
gold bar, his sons and daughters, his cattle,
donkeys and sheep, his tent and all that he had,
to the Valley of Achor. Joshua said, "Why have
you brought this trouble on us? The LORD will
bring trouble on you today." Then all Israel
stoned him, and after they had stoned the rest,
they burned them.* Joshua 7:24-25

I look like my mom: brown hair, brown eyes, and similar
mannerisms. Add twenty-five years to my life, and we would
look identical. We even share some of the same insecurities
and personality traits.

Isn't it interesting how our children become like us? We
long for them to learn from our mistakes so they don't have
to go through the same things we did. We want their lives to

be free from the sins that held us captive. But often, just the opposite occurs. They follow our lead and make the same mistakes we made.

For an example from the Bible, we can look to Abraham and his son Isaac. Abraham lied to the leaders of the land twice: the first time to Pharaoh, leader of Egypt, the second time to Abimelech, King of Gerar. He told them Sarah was his sister rather than his wife. (See Genesis 12 and 20 for the full stories.)

Just six chapters later, Isaac followed his father's lead. He lied to the Philistines and told them his wife was his sister. Isaac probably thought to himself, *lying worked for my father. Why not try it?* It happened in biblical times—one generation passing down a sin to another generation—and it happens now.

A friend of mine is a third generation eating disorder sufferer; both her grandmother and her mother battled the disorder. Men often struggle with pornography after they've seen their dads view it. One quick look into a sex offender's past often reveals the truth: he was molested as a child. Our children (not always, but frequently) struggle with the same sins, addictions, and faults with which we struggled.

Maybe that's why God commanded the Israelites to kill Achan's entire family. Achan disobeyed the Lord by stealing the devoted things. God clearly told the Israelites not to take anything, but Achan did it anyway. His children, though, didn't do anything wrong. Why did they suffer for Achan's sin?

Though there's no way to know with certainty, I think it

might have been because God knew Achan's children would someday lead the people of Israel astray, just like Achan had. Maybe that's why He took such drastic actions—to make certain Achan's sin died with him.

Granted, just because we struggle with a sin doesn't guarantee our children will struggle as well. Some of them will see our mistakes and learn from them. Nonetheless, we cannot afford to take the chance. Confession is hard, accountability is humbling, and removing temptation can sometimes feel impossible. But these steps are nothing compared to the heartache of watching a child drown in sins we led him to.

Questions for Reflection:

1. What sins have you struggled with in recent years or months?

2. What step can you take today to cleanse your life of these sins?

3. Are there any sins or negative behavior patterns you saw in your parents and now see in yourself? If so, please explain.

Prayer:

Lord, take my life and all the sins that daily fight to overcome me. I want to be addicted to you and you alone. Make me yours, Lord. Amen.

Activities:

Day 1 – Make a list of every sin to which you feel drawn. Then destroy the list as a visual reminder that God can take away these sins.

Day 2 – Talk with your kids about sins they might feel drawn to.

Day 3 – Choose an accountability partner.

Day 4 – Confess at least one sin to someone else (your spouse or accountability partner).

Day 5 – If possible, remove a temptation today. (If you're tempted to overeat, remove sweets. If you're tempted to talk inappropriately to another man through Facebook, delete him as a friend, etc.)

WEEK 12:
CALEB

So on that day Moses swore to me, "The land on which your feet have walked will be your inheritance and that of your children forever, because you have followed the LORD my God wholeheartedly." Joshua 14:9

He lay in his bed, a much thinner man than he had been before. His skin looked pale, and his body was ravaged by disease, but his spirit was still optimistic. He smiled as his family gathered around him. Then, as he drew his final breath, his eyes lit up, and he said, "Here I go." For many people, death is scary. It's something they dread and avoid at all costs. But death wasn't frightening for this man. He had complete peace about eternity because he knew where he was going. As his son told this story twenty years after this man's death, it was clear the memory was still vivid in his mind.

As I think about the legacy I want to leave for my children and grandchildren, I have decided I want to be like this man. I want to be the kind of mom who not only proves to her family she's going to heaven, but also leads them there.

Caleb was this kind of parent. He wasn't the most well-known figure in the Bible. After all, if you lined him up with Noah, Moses, Daniel, and Paul, he'd probably go unrecognized. Compared to these popular Bible characters, Caleb could easily fade into the background. Nonetheless, Caleb was a hero, especially in regard to his family.

When Moses sent the twelve spies into the land of Canaan, all but two of them returned defeated, convinced God could not bring them into the Promised Land. Years later, after the unfaithful Israelites died in the desert, God did defeat their enemies. But He only allowed two of the original Israelites into the land: Joshua and Caleb, the two faithful spies. We'll take a look at Joshua's life in the next devotional; today, let's review Caleb's.

The Israelites witnessed God's power in Egypt. They saw Him send frogs, gnats, and blood into the land. They saw Him take the lives of the Egyptian firstborns, and they saw Him overcome Pharaoh. But when it came time to trust, they forgot. They focused on their fear of the future instead of their history with God.

Look at the Lord's rebuke: "*Your children will be shepherds here for forty years, **suffering for your unfaithfulness**, until the last of your bodies lies in the wilderness*" (Numbers 14:33, emphasis mine). Not one of the unfaithful entered the Promised Land. They caused their children to suffer forty years in a hot, lonely desert. But Caleb's children ... their story is completely different. Instead of suffering in a desert and waiting for their unfaithful father to die, they were allowed to enter the Promised Land with their father beside them. And it was all because of the choice Caleb made to be faithful to the Lord. Caleb's children went to the Promised Land for one reason: because Caleb led them there.

Questions for Reflection:

1. For what do you want your children to remember you?

2. What do you need to do today to leave a positive legacy for your children?

3. What legacy did your parents leave for you? (Even if your parents are still living, think about what they taught you and what you will remember about them when they are no longer living on this earth.)

Prayer:

Father, I want to be remembered for my faithfulness to you—not for my own glory but for yours. I want to be someone who brings praise to you, even after I am no longer on this earth. Make me into that kind of person. Develop within me the characteristics of a woman after your own heart. Amen.

Activities:

Day 1 – Complete the following sentence: "I want people to remember me for ..." Write this on a piece of paper, and keep it in your Bible.

Day 2 – On a poster board, draw your family tree. Enlist your children's help in this project. Think about the legacies of each of the people on your tree.

Day 3 – Write a letter to someone who has encouraged your faith.

Day 4 – Look again at your family tree. Thank each of the people in your family who strengthened your faith. If they are no longer living, thank the Lord for these people.

Day 5 – Talk with your children about heaven today. Ask them what they think it will be like.

Week 13: Joshua

But if serving the LORD seems undesirable to you, then choose for yourselves this day whom you will serve, whether the gods your ancestors served beyond the Euphrates, or the gods of the Amorites, in whose land you are living. But as for me and my household, we will serve the LORD. Joshua 24:15

I struggled with the diaper bag and purse in one arm and my twenty-five pound, hungry child in the other. It was the middle of July, and my outfit was quickly becoming a soggy mess as we waited outside for our name to be called to go in and eat. The gentleman on the bench didn't have to offer me his seat. I wouldn't have been offended if he hadn't. But he chose to act, and his choice made him a hero to me. He was a hero, not because he did something extraordinary or displayed a superpower, but simply because he did something when everyone else did nothing.

He reminds me a lot of Joshua. Joshua didn't have extraordinary faith, but he acted when everyone else stayed put. From the way the Lord spoke to him, you get the impression Joshua was weak. After all, God told him over and over again to be strong and courageous, to be unafraid, and to be encouraged (See Joshua 1:6-9). This guy apparently needed a lot of convincing. He didn't believe in himself, didn't think God could possibly use him, and didn't feel worthy to be Moses' apprentice.

Sound familiar? As women, we rarely give ourselves enough credit. We tend to focus on our flaws and ignore our strengths. We doubt whether God can use us. We question our effectiveness as parents. Sometimes, we even wonder why God chose us for this job. But, like Joshua, the Lord is calling to us: "Be strong and courageous. Do not be discouraged."

And like Joshua, we can answer back, "As for our households, we will serve the Lord." We don't have to have superpowers to be heroes for our families. All we have to do is act when everyone else remains unmoved.

When it's easier to sleep in after a busy Saturday, we can come to church anyway. When all we want to do is rest on the couch after a long day and distract our kids with the television, we can color with them instead. When we want to quit on God because we don't understand why He's not answering our prayers, we can choose to trust regardless. In doing so, we become heroes to our children.

We become heroes to them, just like the man who offered his seat was a hero to me. To an onlooker, he may not have done much. But to me, he was a hero.

Questions for Reflection:

1. Who is someone you consider a hero? Why?

2. Who are your favorite biblical heroes?

3. What did they do that made them heroes?

4. List one specific way you can be a hero to your family this week.

Prayer:

Father in heaven, make me like Joshua—willing to stand for you regardless of what everyone else is doing. Give me courage and strength to be my children's hero. Amen.

Activities:

Day 1 – Make superhero capes with your children. (Use tablecloths, pillowcases, or old fabric.)

Day 2 – Do a heroic act today (like buying a college student's lunch or making a card for a nursing home resident.)

Day 3 – Do something heroic for your husband if you're married. Remember, it doesn't have to be extraordinary—just unexpected or atypical.

Day 4 – Make a list (with your children's help) of heroic acts they can do.

Day 5 – Watch a superhero television show or DVD with your children. Then talk about how we can be superheroes for Jesus.

WEEK 14:
JEPHTHAH

*And Jephthah made a vow to the LORD:
"If you give the Ammonites into my hands,
whatever comes out of the door of my house
to meet me when I return in triumph from the
Ammonites will be the LORD's, and I will
sacrifice it as a burnt offering."* Judges 11:30-31

I snapped. Maybe it was just a bad day, maybe it was that time of the month, or maybe my patience was unusually short. Regardless, my two-year-old son did not deserve my frustration, especially since his only mistake was throwing his snack on the floor. My normally patient self exploded. As soon as he started to cry, I felt it: regret. If only I had kept my mouth shut ... if only I had paused before I reacted, if only ... We've all been there. We've all experienced that feeling of regret.

Maybe you said something you shouldn't have and

watched your toddler crumble into a pool of tears. Maybe you yelled when it wasn't necessary. Or maybe, you completely lost it with your husband for no other reason than that you had a bad day. We've all—at one point or another—done something we regretted.

Jephthah certainly experienced regret. He was one of the Judges whom God used to free the Israelites from captivity. His story is found in Judges 10-12. Before he fought the Ammonites, he made a vow to the Lord. He promised that if God helped him defeat his enemies, he would sacrifice whatever came through the front door of his house.

I've often wondered what Jephthah expected to come through the door upon his arrival. He might have expected a cat or dog or other pet, but he certainly did not expect his daughter. I can't imagine the regret Jephthah must have felt when she walked through that open door.

Whether or not it was right of him to keep his vow is irrelevant to our discussion today. What we want to focus on is our words, those rash comments we make and then regret a few hours later. Wouldn't it be so much better to say only words we have thought through, words we won't later regret? Yes, this is easier said than done, but it's not impossible. I've found two steps to help.

First, we can pray before we speak—simple prayers that allow us the opportunity to slow down and think before we utter something we might regret. We've all heard James' command in James 1:19: *My dear brothers and sisters, take note of this: Everyone should be quick to listen, slow to speak and slow to become angry.* But how many of us do it regularly, especially in the midst of a problem or tense situation?

Another helpful solution is to repeat Ephesians 4:29 throughout the day: *Do not let any unwholesome talk come out of your mouths, but only what is helpful for building others up according to their needs, that it may benefit those who listen.* Jephthah learned this lesson too late. Hopefully we won't.

Questions for Reflection:

1. What is one thing you have said and then regretted?

2. What is the most difficult thing about thinking before you speak?

3. Do you think Jephthah was right or wrong when he fulfilled his vow to the Lord? Why?

4. Why is it important to do what you say you will do? Are there ever times when it is appropriate to break a promise?

Prayer:

Lord, help me to think about my words before I speak. I pray you use my words positively to build up and encourage, not to tear down and destroy. It's so hard sometimes to think before I speak. Help me, God. Amen.

Activities:

Day 1 – Memorize Ephesians 4:29 with your family.

Day 2 – Write an encouraging letter to someone on your church staff.

Day 3 – Hide an encouraging note for your husband to find.

Day 4 – Tell your children five things you love about each of them.

Day 5 – Tell another mother why you appreciate her.

WEEK 15: MANOAH AND HIS WIFE (SAMSON'S PARENTS)

Then Manoah prayed to the LORD: "Pardon your servant, LORD. I beg you to let the man of God you sent to us come again to teach us how to bring up the boy who is to be born."
Judges 13:8

Sometimes I wish the Lord would speak to me as clearly as He did to some people in the Bible. It would make decisions much easier. No more wondering if I made a mistake, no more questioning my spouse on the details of a certain choice, and no more regret over a bad decision.

I wish God would come to me in person and help me with my problems like He did with Manoah and his wife. When an angel told them they would soon be pregnant, Manoah prayed to God, *"Pardon your servant, LORD. I beg you to let the man of God you sent to us come again to teach us how to bring up the boy."* God did it, just as they asked. He sent His angel back to them to tell them how to raise their son Samson.

What I have to remember is, even though God probably won't come to me in physical form like He did for Samson's parents, He didn't leave me empty-handed. If I'm willing to search, I'll find that for which I'm looking. The problem is, I'm usually not willing. On a good day, I might spend twenty minutes in Bible study and five minutes in prayer. Then I wonder why God hasn't given me all the answers.

Proverbs 2:3-5 says, *Indeed, if you call out for insight and cry aloud for understanding, and if you look for it as for silver and search for it as for hidden treasure, then you will understand the fear of the LORD and find the knowledge of God.* On most days, I don't search God's Word like it's hidden treasure. My guess is, I'm not alone.

As mothers, we're overworked. Some of us are working two jobs—one at the office, the other at home. We don't stop running until our tired heads hit the pillow at 11 p.m. Even if we stay at home with our children, we're still exhausted. We can't even go to the bathroom without a little one banging on the door. How are we supposed to find quiet, undisturbed time with God?

I'll never claim it's easy. It's not. Finding time for Bible study and prayer is one of the most difficult parts of being a parent. Our time is limited, and our schedules are packed. Nonetheless, the effort we give to Bible study is worth it. When Manoah asked the Lord for guidance, God gave it. He'll do the same for us ... as long as we'll treat His Word like hidden treasure and participate in the search.

Questions for Reflection:

1. What have you learned so far from your study of parents of the Bible?

2. How much time each day do you spend searching God's Word?

3. What steps can you take to lengthen this amount of time?

Prayer:

God, you have provided us with your Word. In it, you have given us all the wisdom we could ever need. Help us make time for you in our busy schedules. When we think we don't have time to read your Word, remind us of time-wasters we could sacrifice for you. Amen.

Activities:

Day 1 – Spend thirty minutes reading your Bible today. Underline, pray, and dig into it.

Day 2 – Develop a study plan you will start upon completion of this book.

Day 3 – Tell the women you meet with weekly one thing God is teaching you through His Word.

Day 4 – Ask each of your children what his/her favorite Bible story is and why.

Day 5 – Spend at least ten minutes in prayer.

WEEK 16:
NAOMI

*Then Naomi said to her two daughters-in-law,
"Go back, each of you, to your mother's home.
May the LORD show you kindness, as you have
shown kindness to your dead husbands and
to me. May the LORD grant that each of you
will find rest in the home of another husband."
Then she kissed them goodbye and they wept
aloud.* Ruth 1:8-9

A mother-in-law causes problems. At least that's the stereotype. Take the television show *Everybody Loves Raymond,* for example. Poor Debra can't do anything right in the eyes of Ray's mom. Marie meddles in her life, gives advice when none is requested, and creates tension between Ray and Debra. She fits the stereotype of a dreaded mother-in-law perfectly.

She is the exact opposite of Naomi, Ruth's mother-in-law. Naomi's story is found in the book of Ruth. By her sacrificial behavior, she proved that not every mother-in-law is a curse. Some, in fact, are great blessings. Unlike the stereotypical mother-in-law, Naomi put her desires below the needs of her in-laws. She wanted what was best for them, even if it wasn't her preference.

Can you imagine how she must have felt when her husband and sons died? She lived in a land away from family, away from friends, and away from the comforts of home. When the men in her life died, she was all alone. Her daughters-in-law were quite literally all she had left. Nonetheless, she encouraged them to return to their families. Not because she wanted them gone, but because she wanted what was best for them.

We follow Naomi's example when we do what's best for our kids regardless of our own desires. In those first few months after my sons were born, I pled for sleep. I prayed God would help them sleep through the night. I even told my boys I would be a better mother if they let me sleep longer. Pathetic, I know. There were times when I didn't want to get up with my babies, but I did it anyway. After all, that's part of being a parent—sacrificing what we want because of what they need.

Sacrifice is difficult. Before having children, I didn't realize how hard it would be to give up my plans and desires. I mistakenly assumed sacrifice would come naturally. That I would want to give up everything for my kids. Then of course, I had children and realized how selfish I was. There were days when I didn't want to play yet another game of peek-a-boo. There were days when all I wanted to do was browse Facebook or dig into a great novel. There were days when it took everything within me to put my desires behind my child's.

Naomi reminds us of what matters most in life—not getting our own desires met but meeting the needs of those around us.

Questions for Reflection:

1. What do you think your child needs most from you today?

2. When have you put your child's needs before your desires? How did this make you feel?

3. Why do you think our culture often views mothers-in-law negatively?

4. Describe your mother-in-law. Does she fit the stereotype or break the mold?

5. What type of mother-in-law do you want to be? List five characteristics you want to display.

6. What do you need to do today to develop these qualities?

Prayer:

Father, ever since the day my children were born, you have been training me to be selfless—to put other people before myself. But it is still very difficult at times. As my children grow and become less dependent on me, it becomes easier to choose myself. Help me to continue to put their needs first. Give me a selfless heart. Amen.

Activities:

Day 1 – Take an entire day to spend with your child. Put all chores aside. Refuse to check Facebook or Twitter or Pinterest or your favorite blog. Make him or her your number one priority today.

Day 2 – Write an encouraging letter to your in-laws.

Day 3 – Spend 30 uninterrupted minutes with each child.

Day 4 – Make two lists: one for your needs and one for your wants. Rebalance your priorities as needed.

Day 5 – Sacrificing for your child doesn't mean you need to neglect your genuine needs such as sleep, food, exercise, and rest. Take time for yourself today.

Week 17:
Hannah

"I prayed for this child, and the LORD has granted me what I asked of him. So now I give him to the LORD. For his whole life he will be given over to the LORD." And he worshiped the LORD there. 1 Samuel 1:27-28

For most of my young adult years, I wanted one thing more than anything else: to have children of my own. Now that I have kids, though, I've realized something. My children are not really mine. Yes, I'm the one who is raising them. But ultimately, they are God's children. He loaned them to me for a few short years. Psalm 100:3 says it this way: *"Know that the LORD is God. It is he who made us, and* **we are his** *..."* (emphasis mine).

Hannah understood this well. She prayed to the Lord for a child, just like we often do.

But then, when God granted her desire, she did something few of us would have strength to do today: she gave him back. Literally. She sent him to live in the temple. She recognized that Samuel was not hers to cuddle and keep close to her side. God gave Samuel to her on loan, and it was her duty to give him back.

Have you ever had a friend borrow something and then return it broken, or worse yet, never return it at all? That's not how God's loan is supposed to work. He gave us our children to care for while we have them, and He expects us to return them someday—not broken but whole.

We might feel unqualified or question our abilities, but God doesn't. He could have done it differently, but He chose to use us because He trusts us. He made the loan, for better or for worse. Now it's our job to care for God's most precious possessions—those little children who call us Mommy.

Can you imagine how Hannah must have felt to give her only child away? I don't know if I could do it. I would probably try to keep him a little longer: "Lord, I'll give him to you when he turns eighteen. Just give me a few more years with him. That way, I can train him more fully." But not Hannah. She recognized Samuel was not hers to keep. He was God's and would therefore be returned to his rightful owner.

Someday we'll have the opportunity to return our children as well, whole and complete, to the arms of their heavenly Father. It's an important task—this job of raising God's children—but the Lord trusts us with it.

Questions for Reflection:

1. Have you ever loaned something to someone and received it back in poor condition? How did this make you feel?

2. How does knowing your children are God's affect the way you raise them?

3. What are the three most important things you want to teach your children in the short time you have them?

Prayer:

Lord, I know my children are yours. You have loaned them to me. Guide my words and actions so that someday, when my time on earth is finished, I can give them back to you with pride. Amen.

Activities:

Day 1 – In question three, you listed three things you want to teach your children. Outline how you will teach them these lessons.

Day 2 – List the qualities you think God sees in you that make you a good parent.

Day 3 – Plan an overnight trip for your children—at a friend's house or with their grandparents—to practice letting go.

Day 4 – Plan the next week's meals. Try to be as healthy as possible.

Day 5 – Get outside with your child today.

WEEK 18:
ELI, PART 1

*"Why do you scorn my sacrifice and offering
that I prescribed for my dwelling? Why do you
honor your sons more than me by fattening
yourselves on the choice parts of every offering
made by my people Israel?"* 1 Samuel 2:29

I admit it. I'm a people-pleaser. I hate being the bad guy
and would rather someone else be the bearer of bad news.
I wonder if Eli felt the same way. Based on this story in 1
Samuel, I think he might have. Let's take a look at what
happened.

Eli was a priest at the Lord's temple. His two sons,
Hophni and Phinehas, were also priests before the Lord.
God placed these young men in leadership, but they took
advantage of their position. When people brought offerings,
Hophni and Phinehas took a portion of the offerings
intended for the Lord and kept it for themselves. They also
slept with the women who served at the Tent of Meeting.

Eli, to his credit, rebuked them. Unfortunately, he didn't do enough to correct their behavior. In 1 Samuel 2, the Lord asked Eli, *"Why do you honor your sons more than me?"* Apparently, Eli didn't want to be the bad guy or the one to create conflict with his kids. He wanted to keep his sons happy, even when it meant breaking the Lord's command.

I wonder how often I do the same thing by ignoring sinful behavior in my children. After all, it's easier to let it go. I find myself thinking (especially after a long and difficult day), *I'll do it tomorrow. It's not a battle I want to fight today.* Unfortunately, all too often, tomorrow never comes. The discipline is left undone. And like Eli, I honor my sons more than my God.

There are instances, of course, when we should choose our battles (like when a child's behavior isn't defiance but is instead a symptom of a need that hasn't been met). Maybe your child is acting out because he's hungry or tired. Or maybe he's simply acting like a normal two-year-old. In these cases, it's not a bad idea to let some things go.

At other times, though, the misbehavior is a big deal and needs to be dealt with. In these instances, it's our duty to discipline. It's our duty to do everything in our power to raise our children into holy men and women. To do this, we have to discipline them even when it's difficult, address sinful behavior in their lives, and love our God more than we love anyone else. Sometimes, this means we have to be the bad guy.

Questions for Reflection:

1. What makes discipline difficult?

2. In what ways has the Lord disciplined you?

3. How is discipline an act of love to your children?

4. How do we sometimes honor our children above God?

Prayer:

Father, you have disciplined me—not out of anger but out of love. I want love to be my motivation as well. Help me control my emotions when I discipline my children. Guide my words so my kids always recognize my love. Amen.

Activities:

Day 1 –Spend time this week researching various methods of discipline.

Day 2 – If you are married, discuss discipline methods with your spouse.

Day 3 – Is there a sinful behavior (such as selfishness, discontentment, or dishonesty) in your children that you need to address? Plan how you will approach them about this sin in their lives.

Day 4 – Is there a sinful behavior in your life? Pray about it.

Day 5 – Talk with your spouse (if you're married) about how your parents disciplined you as a child. Was it effective? Why or why not?

WEEK 19:
ELI, PART 2

A third time the LORD called, "Samuel!" And Samuel got up and went to Eli and said, "Here I am; you called me." Then Eli realized that the LORD was calling the boy. 1 Samuel 3:8

God called Moses from a burning bush (Exodus 3), Gideon from a winepress (Judges 6), Peter from a boat (Matthew 4), Zacchaeus from a life of sin (Luke 19), and Samuel from his bed (1 Samuel 3). His call rarely looked the same twice. For some, it was audible. For others, the call was less apparent—through the words of a prophet or an invitation from a friend.

For most of our children, that's how they will feel the call of God on their lives. They will probably not hear an audible voice, but will instead feel His call in less apparent ways. They might feel God leading them in a certain direction because of the strengths and abilities He has given them or because of their spiritual gifts. God might get their attention through the words of a beloved minister or mentor, maybe even through you.

Thus, it is our job to listen for God's call to our children. In our text for today, Eli recognized God's call to Samuel when Samuel couldn't yet understand it. You'd think a priest would recognize God's call instantly and run at the first word from the Lord. But for Eli, it took three calls to get his attention. God called Samuel three times before Eli recognized God's voice, but at least he recognized it.

It might take a few calls for us as well. But as long as we're listening, God will keep calling. He'll often give us insight into our children's abilities before they recognize it in themselves. They might not be able to see their own strengths, but we can.

Don't let their age fool you. God is calling them—not for future service, but for service now. When my son Rylan was only two years old, he already enjoyed service. One night after my husband got home from work and took his shoes off, Rylan picked the shoes up and put them next to the door (something my husband tends to forget). "Pick up," he said as he ran past me with the shoes that were half his size. If my two-year-old could already serve at such a young age, anyone can.

1 Timothy 4:12 makes it clear God wants to use everyone, regardless of age: *Don't let anyone look down on you because you are young, but set an example for the believers in speech, in conduct, in love, in faith and in purity.* God is calling our kids to make a difference. When they can't

seem to decipher His call on their lives, we should listen. Eli was able to hear God's call to Samuel even when Samuel couldn't, and it could be the same for us.

Questions for Reflection:

1. What strengths and abilities do you see in your children?

2. What do your children enjoy doing?

3. How might God use these hobbies to lead them to His purpose for their lives?

4. What spiritual gifts do you see in your children?

5. What do you feel God called you to do in this life? How did you first recognize His call?

Prayer:

Lord, you are calling each of us to something. Help us listen. When we are so busy we can't hear you, help us slow down. When our minds are overwhelmed with thoughts, empty them and then fill us with your Word. Help us hear you on a daily basis. Amen.

Activities:

Day 1 – Do a Spiritual Gifts Analysis. Contact your local church or look online to find one.

Day 2 – If your children are old enough, help them complete a Spiritual Gifts Analysis as well. If they aren't yet old enough, pray that God will make their gifts known to you soon.

Day 3 – Play Telephone with your children today. Pass a message through whispers, and see how the message is translated with the last person.

Day 4 – Spend five minutes in complete silence, and listen for the Lord.

Day 5 – Play the quiet game with your children. See who can be quiet the longest.

WEEK 20:
SAUL

Saul told his son Jonathan and all the attendants to kill David. But Jonathan had taken a great liking to David. 1 Samuel 19:1

Diann called her five children to her lap and whispered into each of their ears, "Be there." She knew she was dying and that her battle with cancer would soon be over. She wanted each of her children to join her in heaven someday, so she spoke these final words of encouragement to her beloved kids.

She could have been bitter, angry, and selfish in those final weeks. To be honest, no one would have blamed her. It would have been completely understandable for her to be angry with God or distraught over not getting to see her children grow up. But she wasn't. Even in the midst of her own pain and fears, she thought of her family and their eternal futures.

Contrast her with King Saul. They couldn't be more different. While Diann thought of her family first, Saul thought only of himself. This could not be more evident than in Saul's attempts to murder David. Saul was willing to kill David even though he was his son's best friend (1 Samuel 19:1). He was willing to use his daughter as bait (1 Samuel 18:17). He was even willing to kill his own son when Jonathan stood up for David (1 Samuel 20:30-33). Saul would do anything to stop David from stealing the kingdom—even when it meant hurting his own children. He thought only of himself and no one else.

Part of being a parent is learning to think of others. It starts that first night home from the hospital. I think my husband and I got about three solid hours of sleep that night. I was a hormonal mess, near tears for weeks, maybe longer. (The days still blur together.) But it was worth it. If I had the chance to do it all over again, I wouldn't change a thing. Because everything we lost—sleep, time to ourselves, and sanity—was worth it. Where else but in parenting can we enjoy a sloppy toddler kiss? Where else but in parenting can a baby's smile light up our day? Where else but in parenting can we impact young lives for eternity? Few other jobs make such an impact.

Diann recognized her important role as a mother. She knew that even in her final moments, life wasn't about her. In life and in death, she led her family to the Lord. I want to be a mom like that, a mom who leads her kids to the throne regardless of my own circumstances.

Questions for Reflection:

1. Who has inspired you with his/her selfless attitude? Why?

2. When is it important to put yourself first?

3. When is it important to put yourself last?

4. How can you change your routine so you have time for yourself and also time for your family?

Prayer:

Lord, make me a servant. You have provided me with a perfect example—Jesus Christ. Help me to follow him. Transform me into the person you desire me to become, someone who thinks of others first without neglecting myself. Amen.

Activities:

Day 1 – Thank your parents for the sacrifices they made for you. Even if you didn't have the greatest childhood, try to find at least one thing for which you can thank your parents.

Day 2 – In your journal, make a list of the things you love most about being a parent.

Day 3 – Tell your children why you love being their mom.

Day 4 – Take an hour for yourself today.

Day 5 – Have a family night. Order pizza, watch a movie, play a game, or do whatever your family enjoys together.

WEEK 21:
DAVID, PART 1

David noticed that his attendants were whispering among themselves, and he realized the child was dead. "Is the child dead?" he asked. "Yes," they replied, "he is dead." Then David got up from the ground. After he had washed, put on lotions and changed his clothes, he went into the house of the LORD and worshiped. Then he went to his own house, and at his request they served him food, and he ate. 2 Samuel 12:19-20

Over the past couple of years, my husband and I have lost four babies to miscarriage. I'll never get to hold these children, I'll never get to cuddle with them or hear them laugh, and I'll never get to wipe tears from their faces. But I'm glad God will. I hurt for my husband, for me, and for the family who will never get to hold them. But I don't hurt for the babies. They have the best Father anyone could ask for. He'll never make a mistake and never lose His temper. He'll be a better parent than I ever could be.

Right after our first miscarriage, I made a promise to God that I would not let Satan win. I would still worship God, even in the midst of pain. I have kept my promise (often through tears), but I have kept it.

David also worshiped after he lost a child. Granted, his circumstances were different. We did nothing to cause our miscarriages. (And, if you have ever miscarried a child, you need to know you also did nothing to cause yours.) David's son died as a direct result of his sin with Bathsheba. Second Samuel 12:16-18 tells his story: *David pleaded with God for the child. He fasted and spent the nights lying in sackcloth on the ground. The elders of his household stood beside him to get him up from the ground, but he refused, and he would not eat any food with them.*

On the seventh day the child died. David's attendants were afraid to tell him that the child was dead, for they thought, "While the child was still living, he wouldn't listen to us when we spoke to him. How can we now tell him the child is dead? He may do something desperate." God didn't save David's child, regardless of how much David prayed. Nonetheless, David still worshiped. He trusted his God in spite of his pain.

Job is another biblical character who worshiped after losing a child. Even when all ten of his children were killed, he still managed to worship: *At this, Job got up and tore his robe and shaved his head. Then he fell to the ground in worship* (Job 1:20). Later he asked his wife, *"Shall we accept good from God, and not trouble?"* (Job 2:10).

I don't know why God allowed all of our miscarriages. I also don't know why He has allowed the pain in your life, whatever its source may be. What I do know is this: our pain does not change our need to worship. Our God is still God, even when we hurt.

I used to wonder if my faith was strong enough to worship through the death of a child. Now I know the answer. It is. Because of heaven and the promise that God will make all things new, I don't have to wait for my circumstances to change before I get on my knees. After all, true worship isn't about our circumstances anyway. It's about our God's character.

Questions for Reflection:

1. Have you ever lost a child? If so, please journal about this difficult time.

2. How can honesty with God about your questions and doubts help the healing process?

3. Why does God allow His people to experience pain?

4. How can God use your pain to minister to someone else?

Prayer:

Father, you know how it feels to lose a child. You know the ache that never seems to pass and the tears that never seem to stop. I pray for all who have ever lost a child and for any other moms who are hurting for whatever reason—that you give them hope and healing and enable them to worship you in their pain. Amen.

Activities:

Day 1 – Brainstorm how God might want to use your pain to help someone else.

Day 2 – Approximately one in three to four pregnancies end in miscarriage. Chances are, one of your friends has lost a child. Write an encouraging note to her.

Day 3 – If you have lost a child, do something to remember him/her. (Some examples: buy a figurine, write the child a letter, frame a picture or ultrasound image, etc.)

Day 4 – Spend time thanking God for each of the children you have.

Day 5 – Worship your Father today, even in the midst of a difficult circumstance.

WEEK 22:
DAVID, PART 2

*After removing Saul, he made David their king.
God testified concerning him: "I have found
David son of Jesse, a man after my own heart;
he will do everything I want him to do."* Acts
13:22. See also 2 Samuel 12-18 and 1 Kings 1.

David is one of my heroes, a man after God's own heart.
God said of him, *"He will do everything I want him to do."*
When everyone else was afraid of Goliath, he trusted his
God to deliver him (see 1 Samuel 17). When everyone else
thought he should kill his enemy Saul, he refused (see 1
Samuel 24). David wasn't sinless, but he loved his God and
proved it through his obedience. He was as close to perfect
as any other biblical hero.

Nonetheless, even with his successes, David struggled.
Second Samuel describes failure after failure in David's family
life. It all began when David's son died because of David's

affair with Bathsheba. (We talked about this incident in last week's devotion.) Then another son, Amnon, raped David's daughter and faced the rage of her brother, Absalom. After Absalom murdered Amnon, David struggled for years to forgive him, as I'm sure any father would. He forced his child into exile and refused to be in his presence. Years later, Absalom (and then another son, Adonijah) tried to steal David's kingdom. Don't you feel bad for David? Poor guy. I imagine he questioned his parenting skills more than a time or two. *I can control a kingdom, but not my own children. What am I doing wrong?*

Sound familiar? We might not have the same parenting issues as David (at least, I pray we don't!), but we still struggle. Yesterday was one of those days at my house. My words fell on closed ears. My oldest child whined all day long—first because he didn't want to take his pajamas off, then because he didn't want his breakfast. He was unhappy, and I was unhappy. I thought to myself, *am I doing anything right? What is the problem today?*

At least I'm not alone. If David, the man after God's own heart, struggled with his children, we can be sure we will too. Thank the Lord we can still be women after God's own heart, despite our failures and difficulties. David was God's man, even when his family life was far from perfect. We can be God's women too.

Questions for Reflection:

1.   Have you ever questioned your abilities as a
      parent? If so, please describe.

2. Why do you think David struggled so much with his children? Do you think it was because of something he did or didn't do? Explain your answer.

3. What qualities do you think made David a man after God's own heart?

4. What do you need to do today to become a woman after God's own heart?

Prayer:

Lord, parenting is hard. David faced difficulties with his children. You know more than anyone else that I struggle too. Encourage me when I feel defeated, and guide my words and actions so I become a woman after your own heart. Remind me of my potential when I fail. Amen.

Activities:

Day 1 – Decorate paper hearts with your children. Then display them in your home as a reminder to strive to be a woman after God's own heart.

Day 2 – List five qualities you think make someone a person after God's own heart.

Day 3 – Talk with another mother about a current parenting struggle.

Day 4 – You are a great mother. Some days, you just need to tell yourself that. Repeat it five times aloud.

Day 5 – How can your husband (if you're married) encourage you? Tell him one specific way he can support your efforts.

WEEK 23:
JEROBOAM

At that time Abijah son of Jeroboam became ill, and Jeroboam said to his wife, "Go, disguise yourself, so you won't be recognized as the wife of Jeroboam. Then go to Shiloh. Ahijah the prophet is there—the one who told me I would be king over this people." 1 Kings 14:1-2

When life is smooth, I sometimes forget about God—I get wrapped up in the things I have going on and don't come to Him like I should. On the other hand, if something goes wrong, I'm quick to turn to God for help. When a crisis arrives, it's almost natural for me to pray. How sad that it takes a tragedy to get me on my knees. Unfortunately, I doubt I'm alone in this tendency.

Jeroboam certainly struggled with it. His story begins in 1 Kings 11 when Ahijah the prophet told him he would be the king of Israel: *See, I am going to tear the kingdom out of Solomon's hand and give you ten tribes . . . I will do this because they have forsaken me and worshiped Ashtoreth the goddess of the Sidonians, Chemosh the god of the Moabites, and Molek the god of the Ammonites, and have not walked in obedience to me, nor done what is right in my eyes, nor kept my decrees and laws as David, Solomon's father, did* (1 Kings 11:31-33).

Life was good for Jeroboam. He was the King of Israel, after all. God had taken the kingdom from Solomon and handed it over to him, just as the prophet promised. But rather than thank the Lord for His generosity, Jeroboam turned away from Him and worshiped other gods. He made two golden calves and told the people, *"It is too much for you to go up to Jerusalem. Here are your gods, Israel, who brought you up out of Egypt"* (1 Kings 12:28). Jeroboam turned his back on the One who gave him the throne.

Then, when tragedy hit and his son became ill, he came back to God. I think, deep down, he knew God was the only One who could heal his son. Even though Jeroboam hadn't trusted God in his day-to-day life, he turned to Him in times of trouble.

To my shame, I'm often similar to Jeroboam in this. Most days, I rarely think about God. Sure, I think about Him as I read my Bible and pray in the morning. But after that, I go on with my day and allow the distractions of life and motherhood to keep my mind occupied. Then, when a crisis arrives, I run to God in tears.

What I fear is that my kids will learn from my example and only come to God when something bad happens. I don't want my children to view God as some type of genie in a bottle. Just rub the bottle whenever we need something, and God comes running. Rather, I want them to view God as a friend, someone they talk with daily, whether life is going well or sending storms.

God didn't grant Jeroboam's request. And it's really no surprise. Jeroboam had turned his back on God, taken his life into his own hands, and led the people of Israel astray. Sometimes God won't grant our requests either. Maybe not because of our sins as in the case with Jeroboam, but He still might not give us what we want all the time. When this happens and God says "no," I pray I'm able to look at God as my friend, not as a genie of my own creation.

Questions for Reflection:

1. In what ways do Christians sometimes act like God is their genie in a bottle?

2. How often do you pray?

3. About what do you most often pray?

4. What hinders your prayer life? What steps can you take today to rid your life of these hindrances?

5. How can you teach your children to pray?

Prayer:

Lord, I want to be your friend. I don't want to come to you only in times of trouble. Rather, I want to be with you all day long—as I do my daily chores, as I drive to work, and as I talk to my children. Center my mind on you all day every day. Amen.

Activities:

Day 1 – On a sheet of paper or poster board, write positive attributes of God—everything you can think of. If your children are old enough to participate, ask for their help. Display the list in your home.

Day 2 – Create a blessing jar. Every day this week (and longer if you want), write at least one blessing on a sheet of paper and put it in the jar. Use this jar to remind you of God's blessings throughout each day.

Day 3 – Turn your vehicle into a place of worship by filling it with some of your favorite worship CDs.

Day 4 – In question four, you listed steps to improve your prayer life. Take action today.

Day 5 – Look at the list you made on day one. Thank God for each of these attributes.

WEEK 24:
WIDOW AT ZAREPHATH

"As surely as the LORD your God lives," she replied, "I don't have any bread ..." Elijah said to her, "Don't be afraid ... Make a small loaf of bread for me from what you have and bring it to me, and then make something for yourself and your son. For this is what the LORD, the God of Israel, says: 'The jar of flour will not be used up and the jug of oil will not run dry until the day the LORD sends rain on the land.'" She went away and did as Elijah had told her. So there was food every day for Elijah and for the woman and her family. 1 Kings 17:12-15

When my husband and I were first married, I don't know how we paid the bills every month. We were both college students. I worked part time—two days a week—and my husband, Keith, worked at a local furniture store. Somehow, the Lord stretched our money and provided in ways we never would have imagined.

Once, when we were wondering how we would put gasoline in our car, someone left five dollars in our mailbox at school—just enough to get us to our next paycheck. (That was back when gas wasn't nearly as expensive as it is now!) We never went hungry, though we did resort to Ramen noodle meals a time or two. God took care of our needs.

In those lean years, I longed for the day we could stop living on a budget. I couldn't wait until we made enough money to stop watching every penny we spent. I've now learned that day will probably never come. Budgeting is a necessary drudgery, something we'll do even if we make more money. In a weird way, it gives us freedom. When I need a haircut, the money is there because we set aside a small amount every month. When we need new tires or light bulbs, we have the money budgeted so as not to be caught off guard.

On the other hand, budgeting can make spontaneous giving difficult. We budget for giving, but if something unexpected comes up, we might not have the extra money available. For instance, if someone delivers a baby and I want to provide a meal for her family, that money has to come from somewhere. Do I take it from our grocery money and then just hope God stretches what's left? I'm often torn between wanting to give to others and wanting to keep for my family.

The widow at Zarephath faced this same dilemma, but in a more severe way. She was running out of food and getting ready to prepare her family's final meal. Then, Elijah the prophet stepped in and requested she make him some bread. I would have been tempted to tell him no. "Sorry, we just can't help you today. We don't have enough to share." The widow, though, didn't do this. She gave what little she had to Elijah and trusted God would provide for her family. Her faith was incredible. Her family was literally dying of hunger when she gave away their final meal.

God provided for her, and He'll provide for us too. It might mean we have to give up something or adjust the month's budget. It might mean someone else will bless our family in return. We don't have to understand how; we simply have to trust and obey. In doing so, we teach our children God will provide. The widow's son certainly learned of God's faithfulness when she gave out of her need. I wonder how my son will ever learn if I only give out of my plenty.

Questions for Reflection:

1. Describe a time in your life when finances were tight. How did God help you through this difficult time?

2. What are the pros and cons to budgeting?

3. When have you seen God's faithfulness in regard to finances?

4. How does your generosity teach your children to be generous?

Prayer:

Father, you are my provider. You can make my money go much further than I can. Help me to trust you. Give me a generous spirit so I can teach my children about your faithfulness. Amen.

Activities:

Day 1 – Check out Dave Ramsey's website: www. daveramsey.com. Consider taking his Financial Peace University class.

Day 2 – Work to develop a budget. Begin by tracking your income and expenses for the next three months. (For other money-saving tips, check out Appendix C of this devotional. Also, if you'd like more help with your budget, I have a free ebook called *Financial Freedom on a Fixed Income* that I give to all of my newsletter subscribers. You can sign up at my website: www.lindseymbell.com.)

Day 3 – Give something away today (not something you don't need anymore, but something you would still like to keep).

Day 4 – Help each of your children give something away.

Day 5 – Prayerfully consider an organization or missionary your family could begin supporting.

WEEK 25:
A WIDOW & A SHUNAMMITE WOMAN

As the body without the spirit is dead, so faith without deeds is dead. James 2:26. See also 2 Kings 4:1-37.

For fifteen years, a friend of mine fought a nicotine addiction. She hid it from her friends, from her family, and even from her doctors. She tried to quit numerous times but was never successful and returned to cigarettes each time. This all changed when she finally stopped trying to do it on her own strength and instead gave it to God. She can't explain it scientifically, saying instead, "It's truly a God thing. I tried to do it too many times on my own."

Sometimes God doesn't make any sense. We can't explain how He works in our lives, but the evidence of His movement is undeniable.

Such was the case with two parents in 2 Kings 4. The

widow in verses one through seven gathered jars to pay the bills simply because that's what God's prophet told her to do. I think I would have questioned Elisha. "Jars, really? Isn't there any money you can give me instead?" The widow, though, didn't ask questions. She trusted Elisha and obeyed, even though her actions seemed ridiculous, and God rewarded her obedience. After she gathered all the jars and filled them with oil, Elisha said to her, *"Go, sell the oil and pay your debts. You and your sons can live on what is left"* (2 Kings 4:7).

The Shunammite woman in verses eight to thirty-seven likewise trusted even when it didn't make any sense. Her son was dead. To onlookers, all hope was gone. Why bother the prophet now? When the world told her to move on, she persisted and never gave up hope. Her trust in the Lord paid off when Elisha raised her son to life again.

Both of these parents had reason to doubt. Both could have given up on God. But instead, they chose to trust, even when trusting wasn't logical. That's what I'm encouraging you to do today as well: trust God even when it doesn't make a whole lot of sense.

We do this when we give a portion of our income to the Lord, even though we're struggling to pay the bills. We do it when we refuse to take a job because the management won't allow us to have Sunday mornings off for church. We do it when we walk out of an inappropriate movie, even though it cost us twenty dollars. We do it when we believe the Lord can heal our addictions, even when all evidence demands a different conclusion. God's ways sometimes don't make sense. But it's not our job to understand. It's our job to trust and obey.

We expect our children to trust us when we tell them to hold our hands as we cross the street, keep their fingers out of outlets, or walk (instead of run) near a swimming pool. Our kids might not understand our motives, but we want them to obey regardless. After all, we know best, right? Likewise, we might not understand God's motives. But He, without a doubt, does know best. What will our children learn when they watch us trust the Lord, even when it doesn't make any sense?

Questions for Reflection:

1. When has the Lord led you to do something you didn't understand? Please describe what happened.

2. Why is it difficult to trust when we don't understand?

3. How has the Lord blessed your obedience in the past? Please be specific.

Prayer:

Father, I want my children to trust me, even when they don't understand. I know they will learn from me, so I pray for you to help me trust you. When you lead me to something I don't understand, help me to obey. Give me the courage and strength to follow, regardless of whether or not your command makes sense to me. Amen.

Activities:

Day 1 – Begin tithing your income to the Lord this week.

Day 2 – Is the Lord leading you to do something today you don't understand? If so, do it anyway.

Day 3 – Do a random act of kindness for someone today.

Day 4 – Write a paragraph about why God is trustworthy. Then read the paragraph aloud.

Day 5 – Do something that might not make sense to a watching world. Pay for a stranger's dinner at a local restaurant. Give up time with your friends to spend time with your family. Do an act of kindness for someone in your neighborhood. The ideas are limitless. Be creative, and have fun.

Week 26:
Kings of Israel and Judah,
Part 1

To this day their children and grandchildren continue to do as their ancestors did. 2 Kings 17:41

A few weeks ago, I took some much-needed time off. For a stay-at-home mom, time off means going somewhere—anywhere—alone. It means doing anything as long as you don't have someone pulling on your shirt saying, "Hold you please. Hold you please." It was wonderful. On my return home, I found my toddler standing in the entryway, wearing Daddy's coat and Daddy's shoes. He was a miniature man and looked just like his father. I couldn't resist snapping a picture, but then I thought about how symbolic the picture was.

Our kids try to look like us, in more ways than one. Yes, they try on our clothes, but they also act like us, take on our characteristics and mannerisms, and maybe even pick up our sins.

The book of Second Kings is not the first place we would typically turn for parenting advice. In fact, it's probably one of the last. The book provides little parenting wisdom and few positive examples. But, there is at least one lesson we can learn. Over and over again, the books of First and Second Kings say words similar to these: "Their children continue to do as their fathers did." Like my son who wanted to look like his father, these kids wanted to be like their dads.

Ahaziah was evil like his father, Ahab, who was evil like his father, Omri. In a similar fashion, Jotham was good like his father, Uzziah, who was good like his father, Amaziah. And Amaziah was good like his dad, Joash. There is no denying it. Parents influence their children in a mighty way—whether it is good or bad. Our children, more often than not, become like us.

I doubt many people would argue with this. They might, however, wonder how to influence their kids in a positive way. Listed below are three practical steps to take today:

1. Be an example. The best way to mold children into servants is to be a servant. The best way to create a selfish child is to think only of yourself. By far, the greatest thing we can do to influence our children positively is to be a positive example.

2. Be positive (especially about things related to God and His Church). Parents often don't realize how much their children listen. Even when kids are watching television or appear to be zoned out, they are likely picking up on a lot of what you say. Choose your words carefully, especially

when talking about the church or God. If all your children hear about church is what's wrong with it, they could develop a negative view of God's people or God Himself.

3. Be involved. Your kids can't learn from you if you're never around. Being there can make all the difference. Quality time is important, but so is quantity time. Your children need to be with you.

Questions for Reflection:

1. Which of the above three steps do you need to improve upon?

2. What other ways can you be a positive influence in your child's life?

3. How did your parents influence you, either in a positive or negative way?

4. If you could only teach your child one lesson, what would you want him or her to learn?

Prayer:

God in heaven, you gave us Jesus as the ultimate example. I desire for Him to influence my life more than anyone else. Mold me into the parent you desire. Help me to influence my children in a positive way, rather than a negative way. Amen.

Activities:

Day 1 – Take a picture of you and your children. Do they look like you?

Day 2 – List five good qualities in yourself you want your children to emulate.

Day 3 – Now list five not-so-good qualities in yourself you don't want your children to copy.

Day 4 – Compare childhood pictures of yourself with pictures of your children. Maybe even make a collage with some of their pictures and some of yours. This can be a fun activity to do with your children, even if they were adopted or look different than you.

Day 5 – Create acrostic poems, using the letters in your children's names to list character traits you want them to display. If your children are old enough, allow them to decorate the poems. Then frame and display them in your home. Use these poems as reminders that your children are following the example you set for them. A sample acrostic poem with the name Matt is below:

M- Modest
A- Always Generous
T- Tender
T- Truthful

Week 27:
Kings of Israel and Judah, Part 2

He did what was right in the eyes of the LORD,
just as his father David had done. 2 Kings 18:3

Kaitlyn didn't know her father. He left when she was a baby. Her mother blamed her for this and never let her forget it. If she started to forget, a black eye or bruised arm reminded her. After reading through the books of First and Second Kings and seeing that most of the kings followed the example of their parents, I wonder ... is Kaitlyn destined to be like her mother—an abusive, angry woman who uses her child as a punching bag?

Just as these biblical books teach us that our children often follow in our footsteps (see Week 26), it also teaches that it's possible to change our family trees. Some of us never knew our parents. Some of us were abused. Others just never felt good enough for love.

Just because our parents failed doesn't mean we have to. We can choose to be different, just like Asa, Joash, Hezekiah, and Josiah did. Each of these kings turned away from the evil behavior of their parents and followed the Lord. They followed the example of David, their forefather, instead of following their actual parents. I've often wondered how they were able to do it. When most of the kings continued the behavior of their parents, how did a handful of them change? What made them different? In last week's devotion, we looked at ways to become positive influencers for our children. Today, we'll look at ways to break away from our parents and choose to be different.

1. Learn from your parents' bad behavior. If your dad yelled at you, choose to vent your anger some other way. Try working out or getting a punching bag. I know of one woman who threw old plates at a tree to vent her frustrations. (Of course, if you decide to try this, make sure and pick up the glass particles!) If your mom criticized most of your attempts at creativity, choose to encourage your child in his efforts. Learn from what your parents did poorly, and choose to behave differently.

2. Recognize the tendency to follow the poor example set by your parents. If you don't identify the temptation, you will likely fall. On the other hand, if you know you tend to be overly critical just like your father, you can take steps to prevent it.

3. Forgive your parents for whatever they did to

hurt you. Your bitterness and anger is hurting you just as much (if not more) than it is hurting your parents. Even if they haven't asked for your forgiveness, give it nonetheless.

4. Look for positive influencers, and find a mentor. If your parents weren't good examples for you, find someone who is, and learn from this person.

Questions for Reflection:

1. Do you know anyone who changed his/her family tree in a positive way? Please explain.

2. What can you do today to change your family tree? Even if you had great parents, there were certainly things they could have done better. Determine today to pass down the great things and improve upon the not-so-great.

Prayer:

God, thank you for being a wonderful Father. Help me overcome any hurt feelings from my parents. Help me learn from their mistakes. Use me to be a positive influence for my children. I want to leave a godly legacy for them. Help me, Lord. Amen.

Activities:

Day 1 – Look back at the family tree you created in Week 12. Do you see any sins or negative behavior patterns your parents or grandparents passed down?

Day 2 – If your parents weren't positive examples, find a mentor who will be.

Day 3 – If you're thankful for the legacy of your parents, find some way to thank them. Send them a gift or a card or do something special for them.

Day 4 – Think of at least one way you can be a better parent. Write it down.

Day 5 – If your parents hurt you as a child, either emotionally or physically, write them a letter explaining your frustrations and anger. Don't hold anything back. This letter is for your benefit, not for their reading. I would recommend you not give it to them.

Week 28:
Men of Judah

"Our God, will you not judge them? For we have no power to face this vast army that is attacking us. We do not know what to do, but our eyes are on you." All the men of Judah, with their wives and children and little ones, stood there before the LORD. 2 Chronicles 20:12-13

On September 13, 1995, my 39-year-old mother got into the baptistery with my two brothers and me. Each of us confessed the Lord as our God and Savior and gave our lives to Him. I imagine that took a lot of courage for my mother. It's one thing to give your life to the Lord when you're little; it's more difficult to do so as an adult with your children watching. With humility, she admitted she couldn't do life on her own. She needed God's help. When I think of all she taught me over the years, this lesson stands out as one of the greatest.

I imagine the children in 2 Chronicles 20 learned this same lesson from their parents. With enemy armies surrounding them, those parents came before the Lord *with their children and little ones.* They could have come alone and left their children at home. I imagine that would have been easier. No crying babies. No squirming children. But instead, they allowed their kids to see humility in action. They allowed them to see people coming before the Lord in brokenness. In doing so, they taught their children it's okay to be broken before the Lord, and it's okay to ask for help.

What I love about this story is that God came through for them. Immediately after they prayed, the Spirit of the Lord came upon one of the men and *he said: "Listen, King Jehoshaphat and all who live in Judah and Jerusalem! This is what the LORD says to you: 'Do not be afraid or discouraged because of this vast army. For the battle is not yours, but God's.'"* (2 Chronicles 20:15).

When we face financial difficulties or relationship problems, it's okay to show a little bit of vulnerability to our kids. They need to see us come to God in brokenness every now and then. Granted, our children don't need to know every detail of every problem we face. That would only breed worry. But, knowing we struggle is healthy. And knowing how we struggle, how we come to the Lord for help, will teach them to lean upon Him as well. I can think of no one better to lean on and no one else who can help like He can. After all, the battle is really not ours anyway; it's His.

Questions for Reflection:

1.   How is transparency with your children a positive thing?

2.   When does transparency become unhealthy?

3.   What is one thing with which you are currently struggling? How could you use this difficulty to teach your children to lean upon the Lord? Please be specific.

Prayer:

Father, you are bigger than all my problems. Help me to bring them to you. Don't allow my fear of looking weak to keep me from coming to you. Teach me to bring everything, whether it is big or small, to your arms because you can carry it all. Amen.

Activities:

Day 1 – This week, pray with each of your children every night. Talk to them about their struggles, and teach them to bring them before the Lord.

Day 2 – Memorize Matthew 11:28 with your children: *Come to me, all you who are weary and burdened, and I will give you rest.*

Day 3 – With your children, bring one concern before the Lord.

Day 4 – Go on a nature walk. Find a flower. Talk to your children about how God takes care of the flower and remind them He'll take care of your family too.

Day 5 – Play a relay game with your children. On one end of the room, create a large pile of toys. On the other end, place a laundry basket. Have your children fill small trash bags with toys, race to the basket and unload, then repeat until all the toys are in the basket. Explain that just as they carried the toys, God can carry our worries for us.

WEEK 29:
ISRAELITES

*After I looked things over, I stood up and said
to the nobles, the officials and the rest of the
people, "Don't be afraid of them. Remember
the Lord, who is great and awesome, and
fight for your families, your sons and your
daughters, your wives and your homes."*
Nehemiah 4:14

We fight with our children, with our spouses, with the computer or washing machine, and with our old car that desperately needs a tune-up. A day rarely passes when I'm not battling with someone or something. But how often do I fight *for* my family? Not with them, but for them.

In our text today, Nehemiah challenged the Israelites to fight for their families: for their brothers, their sons and daughters, their wives, and their homes. The story begins as the Israelites returned to Jerusalem after captivity to find a wreck of a town. Jerusalem was in serious need of repair, so Nehemiah formed a team to rebuild the city's walls. Unfortunately, the neighboring towns tried to stop the work. They didn't want the city of Jerusalem (that was once very powerful) to regain its position. But in spite of opposition, Nehemiah stood strong. *Fight for your families,* he told them.

Our lives are different than the Israelites' lives. We don't have to worry about neighboring towns attacking us as we work to rebuild our city's walls. But the command to fight for our families stands as true today as it did in their day. The application is just different. We're not physically fighting, but the principle is the same. Our enemy wants nothing more than to destroy our marriages and our families. We have to fight back.

One way to fight off Satan's attack is to be intentional about spending time with our families. My favorite memories from my childhood are of family vacations. My parents made it a point to take us somewhere almost every year. Some years it was a day trip to a local amusement park. Other years it was a tag-along trip in which we accompanied my dad on one of his business trips. And then, every so often, we took a big trip to a beach or the mountains. I grew up in Oklahoma, so going to the beach or the mountains was an event for us.

These trips weren't special because of the amount of money we spent. My mom often brought our food in a cooler shoved between the minivan seats, and sometimes we found free or inexpensive activities to enjoy. What made them special was the time we spent together. There's nothing like getting to know one another on a 14-hour car ride.

Another way my parents fought for our family was by

creating weekly family times. In my teen years, my brothers and I took turns choosing a family activity. We played mini-golf, went to the movies, went bowling, went to dinner, or did whatever we chose on our week. The only rule was that no one could complain about the chosen activity.

What we do with our families is not what's most important, as long as we are doing something. After all, if we're not fighting for our families, we will fight with them. And then, I'm afraid Satan might win the battle. Let's not give him the chance.

Questions for Reflection:

1. What is one way you can be more intentional about spending time with your family?

2. What would your children enjoy doing with you? Sometime this week, ask each of them what they would like to do with you. Some ideas include: going fishing, to the park, on a picnic, to a zoo, for a walk, to a baseball game, etc.

Prayer:

Lord, I want to be more intentional about spending time with my family. Help me be creative as I search for inexpensive ways to enjoy their company. Guard my time so I don't allow other things to fill my calendar. Amen.

Activities:

Day 1 – Family activities don't have to cost a lot of money. Search the Internet sometime this week to find free or inexpensive local activities for your family.

Day 2 – Plan a family vacation, and start saving. If you save for several months, maybe even a year, you should be able to have a nice trip without going into debt.

Day 3 – Ban the television for the entire day.

Day 4 – Eat dinner at the table with your family.

Day 5 – From this point forward, designate one night a week as family night. If you need to change the particular night sometimes, that's fine. Just make sure it happens at least once a week. If your children are old enough, allow them to plan the evenings on occasion.

WEEK 30:
MORDECAI

"For if you remain silent at this time, relief and deliverance for the Jews will arise from another place, but you and your father's family will perish. And who knows but that you have come to your royal position for such a time as this?" Esther 4:14

Obstacles are often opportunities in disguise. When I was fifteen years old, I woke one morning with an intense pain in my right foot. I tried to "walk it off" and assumed it was just a sore muscle from the previous day's cheerleading practice. But the pain intensified, so I went to the doctor. I had a bone cyst, a fluid-filled pocket, growing in my foot and eating away at what little bone remained in my heel.

One week later, I had surgery—a painful process in which the doctors removed bone from my hip and transferred it to my foot. As a fifteen-year-old girl getting ready for a cheerleading competition, I was devastated. I couldn't compete in my upcoming competition, I had to walk on crutches, and I needed help with nearly everything I did. For an insecure teenager, it felt like the end of the world.

Nonetheless, God was moving. He was using my obstacle as an opportunity to bring me closer to Him, to re-prioritize my life, and to minister to other people who were hurting. I had never before thought of surgery as a big deal. After having mine, I could empathize with the fears and worries that often accompany a surgical procedure. Surgery is a big deal, and those who are undergoing it need encouragement. My obstacle was my opportunity, but it took awhile for me to realize it.

Mordecai must have known about the hidden blessings of a challenge. He was not Esther's biological parent, but he raised her as his daughter when her parents died. At the time when Esther was queen, a man named Haman went to King Xerxes and requested the entire Jewish nation be destroyed. Haman, as well as King Xerxes, didn't realize Queen Esther was Jewish, so Haman's plot went into effect. On a certain day, all people everywhere were commanded to destroy the Jewish people.

When Mordecai heard of the plot, he challenged Esther to speak to the king. Even though going to him without being called could end her life, and even though challenging him could cost her dearly, Mordecai said to Esther, "*Who knows but that you have come to your royal position for such a time as this?*" (Esther 4:14). He recognized that the lives God calls us to are not always easy or free of challenges. But if we let God work, He can turn any obstacle into an opportunity.

Our children will face challenges too. I wish they wouldn't, but they will. How we react to these challenges is important. Will we tell them to give up and allow them to wallow in self-pity? Or will we, like Mordecai, encourage them to rise above the problem and watch God turn their obstacle into an opportunity?

Questions for Reflection:

1. When has God turned an obstacle into an opportunity in your life?

2. What difficulties are you facing right now? Pray about each of these today.

3. What obstacles are your children facing? Pray about these as well.

Prayer:

God, you can turn any obstacle into an opportunity. You can use anything for your glory. I pray that you would use our struggles. Don't allow them to be in vain. As you used the pain Jesus experienced for your glory, use our pain for your glory as well. Amen.

Activities:

Day 1 – Read *The Very Hungry Caterpillar* by Eric Carle (New York: Philomel Books, 1987) with your children. Talk about how God turns a somewhat ugly caterpillar into a beautiful butterfly. He'll do the same with our problems.

Day 2 – Using markers or crayons, draw butterflies with your children.

Day 3 – Think about a rainbow—another example of God using a storm to make something beautiful.

Day 4 – Create a watercolor rainbow with your children.

Day 5 – Make a list of all the opportunities God has given you. Some might be in the form of obstacles, some in the form of gifts or abilities, and some in the form of weaknesses. How does God want to use you for His glory? Please be as specific as possible.

WEEK 31:
JOB

When a period of feasting had run its course, Job would make arrangements for them to be purified. Early in the morning he would sacrifice a burnt offering for each of them, thinking, "Perhaps my children have sinned and cursed God in their hearts." This was Job's regular custom. Job 1:5

In those first few months after my children were born, my body ached with exhaustion. I tried to adapt to the catnaps between feedings, but any new mom will tell you the adjustment is difficult. You want to sleep but can't, at least not for long enough. The last thing a new mom wants to do in those months is wake up earlier than she has to ... even if it is for something important like prayer.

Looking back now, though, I wish I had spent more time in prayer when my kids were infants—even if it wasn't early in the morning. My relationship with the Lord, with my husband, and probably even with my children suffered because I allowed my prayer life to falter.

Job, in contrast, made prayer a priority. It was his *regular custom* to rise early in the morning and pray for his children. Maybe that's why he was able to face such insurmountable difficulties without turning his back on the Lord. I can think of nothing worse than Job's sufferings. He lost his livestock, his servants, and all ten of his children—all within a few hours. Then, a little while later, he lost his health. All he had left was a wife who encouraged him to give up his faith, curse God, and die.

Nonetheless, *Job did not sin in what he said* (Job 2:10). As I read Job's story, I'm amazed at his faith and can't help but wonder, how did he do it? When his life fell apart, how did he remain hopeful?

I think his prayer life had something to do with it. Job was close to God. He talked to Him on a regular basis. They had a history together, so even when his life fell apart, Job knew better than to curse his Friend and his God. His prayer life gave him strength to persevere.

It's easy to talk about the importance of prayer, but it's much more difficult to make it happen on a regular basis—especially as a busy mother. When our days are packed with diaper changes, ball games, and dance recitals, how do we make time for the Lord and make prayer a *regular custom*, like Job did? Listed below are nine ideas that might make it a little bit easier:

1. First thing in the morning and right before you go to sleep, say a quick prayer.

2. Incorporate sentence prayers into your daily activities. "Lord, give me wisdom to handle ..." "Lord, I'm angry right now. Control my tongue." Etc.

3. Once a week or once a month, write a prayer of encouragement for someone and give it to him/her.

4. Walk around your neighborhood and pray for the individuals living in each of the homes. This works great if you have young children who enjoy going on walks. (Plus, it's a great way to get exercise!)

5. Use the times in your car as divine appointments.

6. Get together with a friend once a week to share prayer requests. If your friend has children, this is a great opportunity to allow your kids to play together.

7. Pray with your kids daily. Once they are talking, allow them to pray. Encourage them to write prayers for other people like you do.

8. Pray while doing mindless activities like mowing, washing dishes, or folding laundry.

9. Designate at least five minutes a day for prayer.

Questions for Reflection:

1. Which of the above ideas will you incorporate into your life?

2. On a scale of 1-10 (10 being very regular, 1 being very irregular) how would you rate your prayer life? What hinders it?

3. What else could you do to strengthen your prayer life?

4. Why is prayer so important?

Prayer:

God, you have given us the privilege of prayer. You are the Creator of the universe—so much bigger than us and so much holier. And yet, you allow us to come to you as friends. We often take this privilege for granted. Forgive us when we don't treasure our time with you, and help us desire you more. Amen.

Activities:

Every day this week, pray for your children. Use the topics listed below as a guide:

Day 1 –Their Love for the Lord

Day 2 – Their Love for Others

Day 3 – Their Future Spouses

Day 4 – Their Future Careers

Day 5 – Their Purity

WEEK 32:
LESSONS IN PSALMS

*Through the praise of children and infants you
have established a stronghold against your
enemies, to silence the foe and the avenger.*
Psalm 8:2

Ever since my boys were toddlers, they have loved to make
music. My husband gave them drumsticks when they
were only a few months old, so of course the drum (and
I might add, the loudest instrument) is their favorite. At
times it's tempting to discourage them when they bang the
drumsticks on a metal pan, especially when I long for quiet
at the end of a chaotic day.

But then I think about these verses: *LORD, our Lord,
how majestic is your name in all the earth! You have set your
glory in the heavens. Through the praise of children and infants
you have established a stronghold against your enemies, to
silence the foe and the avenger* (Psalm 8:1-2). The Lord wants

our children to make music for Him. He wants to hear their off-tempo and off-key songs. It delights His heart.

So, instead of discouraging the loud, sometimes ear-piercing music my children create, I clap and sing along. (Or at least ... I try my best to hide the fact I wish the noise would quiet.) After all, I'm not just encouraging them to make music, but also to worship their Father.

One of the primary ways we worship is through music. By instilling a love of music in our children, we help them enjoy worship in the years to come. But, music is not the only way to worship. Worship is not a Sunday-only activity. It's a lifestyle, a 24-hour-a-day, 7-day-a-week attitude of the heart. So how do we instill *this* in our children?

One way is by helping them use their creativity to worship. If our child likes to draw, we challenge him to draw a biblical story. Not only will he worship through art, but he'll also learn the story. If our child enjoys writing, we provide her a journal to write prayers or short stories. If our child enjoys the outdoors, we create a nature walk and teach him about God's creative abilities. Whatever our children enjoy can be an opportunity for worship if we teach them to worship in the ordinary. Colossians 3:17 reminds us, *And whatever you do, whether in word or deed, do it all in the name of the Lord Jesus, giving thanks to God the Father through him.* Our kids don't have to be in a church building to worship. But it's our job to teach them to worship in the day-to-day things of life.

Another way to develop attitudes of worship in our children is by serving with them. We could deliver handwritten cards to a local nursing home, pass out food at a homeless shelter, or rake the neighbor's yard. Granted, when our children help, the project is likely to take twice as long. Actually, it will probably be more work for us than if our kids hadn't helped. But, the extra time and effort are worth it. I'd rather gain a child with a heart of worship than an hour of my time any day. Wouldn't you?

Questions for Reflection:

1. What do your children enjoy? How could these activities become worship opportunities?

2. What can you do as a family to prepare for Sunday morning worship?

3. In what service opportunities could your family participate? Your church will likely know of local opportunities.

4. What can you do to help instill a love of music in your children?

Prayer:

Lord, you are worthy of worship. Not just on Sundays, but every day. Fill our hearts with adoration for you, and help us instill hearts of worship in our children. We love you and praise you, Lord. Amen.

Activities:

Day 1 – Play musical instruments (real or toy) with your
children.

Day 2 – Get your child's creative juices flowing. Give him
paper and art supplies, and encourage him to
draw a picture for God.

Day 3 – Serve with your children today.

Day 4 – Plan to sit in church together this week (kids and
all). Sometimes we are so busy at church doing our
own things (nursery, youth group, volunteer work,
etc—all good things, by the way!) that we don't
spend time with our family. Let your children see
you worship this Sunday.

Day 5 – Worship with your family at home using your
favorite worship songs.

WEEK 33:
LESSONS IN PSALMS

We will tell the next generation the praiseworthy deeds of the LORD, his power, and the wonders he has done. Psalm 78:4

Somewhere beneath a pile of books and office supplies in my desk lays one of my most treasured possessions: a small black notebook. It's not worth much to anyone else, but to my husband and me, it's a treasure. Every anniversary, we read through the notebook and record the previous year's highlights—job changes, births, moves, new additions to the family, home projects, funny stories, and anything else we don't want to forget. I love looking through the book year after year and remembering from where we've come.

The Israelites used memorials to help them remember too. For instance, in Joshua 4, they set up a memorial to remind their children how God stopped the flood waters of the Jordan River so they could cross from one side to the other. They did this because they didn't want future generations to forget the miracles the Lord had done for them.

The author of Psalm 78 didn't want his children to forget either. *My people, hear my teaching; listen to the words of my mouth. I will open my mouth with a parable; I will utter hidden things, things from of old—things we have heard and known, things our ancestors have told us. We will not hide them from their descendants; we will tell the next generation the praiseworthy deeds of the LORD, his power, and the wonders he has done* (Psalm 78:1-4). This man refused to allow his children to forget about God.

Sometimes I fear we don't have this same determination, though. God is moving in our lives and in the lives of our families, but if we aren't careful, we'll forget about it. Once He helps us through our financial problem, heals our child of his sickness, or repairs a relationship, we'll move on with the busyness of the day. We might be extra thankful for a few days, maybe even a few months, if the Lord did something extraordinary, but eventually, the thankfulness will fade. Unless, of course, we create a memorial—some way to help us remember the goodness of the Lord.

I've listed a few memorial ideas below for you to consider:

1. Journal about the Lord's blessings. You could do this once a year, once a month, once a week, or even once a day. You could even include pictures like a scrapbook.

2. Talk about what God is doing in your life at the

dinner table each night. My husband and I have started doing this with our kids. We take turns sharing both our high and low points for the day.

3. Keep a thankfulness jar in your kitchen. When God blesses you with something, write about it on a slip of paper, and put it in the jar. (I suggested you do something similar to this in Week 23. Have you done it yet? If not, now is the perfect time to start!)

4. Keep a prayer log to record answered prayers.

For me, forgetting about God's goodness is easy. All it takes is one bad day to bring me down. Remembering His blessings isn't quite as easy, but it is worth the effort.

Questions for Reflection:

1. What has the Lord done for you this week? Please be specific.

2. How could you help your family remember the workings of the Lord?

3. How could you create a memorial for your family? (Like the Israelites did when the Lord stopped the Jordan River.) Be creative as you brainstorm. On Day 3, you'll have the opportunity to build this memorial.

4. Which of the above ideas would you like to incorporate into your life?

Prayer:

Father, you do amazing miracles every day. Forgive me when I neglect to notice them. Keep my eyes open to your movement, and help my family remember your goodness. You, Lord, are a good and loving God. May I never forget that. Amen.

Activities:

Day 1 – When could you journal with your family? Once a month? Once a year? Once a day? Make a plan to do so. If you're only doing it once a year, write it on the calendar.

Day 2 – Tell your spouse or children one thing God has done for you this week.

Day 3 – Build a memorial with your children.

Day 4 – Celebrate the goodness of God with a party—cake, candles, and all!

Day 5 – Begin recording this year's memories. Think about life changes, significant purchases, funny incidents, vacations, and maybe even fights that now bring a smile to your face.

WEEK 34:
LESSONS IN PSALMS

Children are a heritage from the LORD,
offspring a reward from him. Psalm 127:3

Today was one of those days I couldn't do anything right. My house was a mess. My children were cranky. My husband and I were on edge with each other. It was one of those days when I wished for a "do over" button. I suspect you've had days like this too—days when you wish you could go back to bed and then start over.

On days like this, it's important to remember why we parent our children. With all of the stress children bring, not to mention the pain of childbirth, lack of sleep, and potty-training nightmares, is it worth it?

I want to reassure you (just in case you are having one of those rough days today) that it is worth it. Think back to that first toothless smile, that first hug, that first time he said, "I love you." I'm sure you would agree that nothing compares. Parenting is worth it—worth all the tears, all the stress, and all the pain. As the psalmist says, blessed is the man who has children. I couldn't agree more (even on days like today).

Children bless our lives by teaching us so many things. First of all, they teach us to be selfless. In those first few months, we learn to put ourselves last by rolling out of bed at one and four a.m. to nourish their helpless bodies. But it doesn't stop at infancy. As the years pass, our children continue to teach us. Not consciously, of course, but through their needs and wants. My parents often sacrificed their desires for my brothers and me. As parents, we forfeit what we want so our kids can get what they desire.

Children also teach us how to trust. When our children are little, before they realize we make mistakes, they trust us completely. We're their heroes. Mommy can make any boo-boo better. Daddy can fix anything. Our kids don't worry, because we take care of everything.

Maybe that's why Jesus said, *Truly I tell you, unless you change and become like little children, you will never enter the kingdom of heaven* (Matthew 18:3). Jesus longs for us to trust Him like our toddlers trust us—with complete abandon.

After bath time each night, my youngest son, Caden, loves to run around without his diaper on, completely naked and unashamed. That's how God wants us to live— not necessarily naked, but unashamed, free of worries, and completely comfortable in the life God gave us. After all, He can make any boo-boo better; He can fix anything. The psalmist was right: children are a reward from the Lord, and we are blessed to have them.

Questions for Reflection:

1. What other lessons have your children taught you?

2. How does each of your children bless your life?

3. What other qualities (along with trust) do our children possess that might have caused Jesus to tell adults to become like children?

4. When do you struggle to trust Jesus? Please be as specific as possible.

5. You've thought about how your children bless your life. How do you bless theirs?

Prayer:

Father in heaven, thank you for blessing my life with children. Even on days when I feel overwhelmed, I know I am blessed. May I be a blessing to my family as they have been a blessing to me. Amen.

Activities:

Day 1 – Tell each of your children why he or she blesses your life.

Day 2 – Tell your spouse (if you are married) how he blesses your life.

Day 3 – Go to a park (weather permitting) and observe the interactions between children. Think about how they trust, how they love, and what they can teach you.

Day 4 – Think of one way you can bless each of your children today.

Day 5 – Now think of one way you can bless your spouse.

WEEK 35:
LESSONS IN PROVERBS

He who gathers crops in summer is a prudent son, but he who sleeps during harvest is a disgraceful son. Proverbs 10:5

When I was a teenager, I loved mowing the lawn. I thought of it as a way to get a tan, listen to music, and be alone. Plus, I got paid. My parents owned five acres, so I could earn quite a bit of cash. At the time, I thought my dad's only motivation was to get someone else to mow so he didn't have to. Now I know he had much more in mind.

He wanted my brothers and me to learn the value of work. Proverbs 10 describes the wise son. He is diligent, he works hard during crop season, and he brings joy to his parents. My dad wanted us to be wise children like the son in these verses.

By providing our children opportunities to make money, we teach them how the world functions. If we don't go to work, we don't get paid. Likewise, if our children don't do their chores, they don't get paid. When they can't buy a candy bar at the grocery store because they don't have any money, they'll learn the value of work.

Of course, some chores should be required because our kids are part of the family and every member needs to contribute. Other chores, though, can be paid duties. As parents, we decide which chores are mandatory, because-you're-part-of-the-family chores, and which ones are commission-based. Maybe making the bed is mandatory, no pay, but vacuuming is done for payment. As much as we might dislike that our society runs on money, it does. So, it's essential we teach our children to work.

It's also important we teach our children how to handle their money once they get it. I'm a natural saver. My husband, on the other hand, is a natural spender. He knows exactly how he will spend his money before he gets it in hand. Our children will likely go one way or the other also. But just because one child is a natural spender doesn't guarantee she will be bankrupt right out of college. And, just because one is a natural saver doesn't guarantee he will hoard his money for himself. With direction, both can learn to save, spend wisely, and give.

One way to teach them is to use the envelope system or a three-part-bank. At every payday, our children divide their money three ways—a portion into savings, a portion into giving, and the rest into spending. Another idea is to open a savings or checking account for our children. Most of our children won't learn how to use money wisely without our help. They're counting on us.

Questions for Reflection:

1. Are you a natural saver or a natural spender? How have you learned to balance your natural tendency?

2. What chores would you like to make commission-based? How much money do you want to pay for each of these chores?

3. What chores would you like to make mandatory, because-you're-part-of-the-family duties?

Prayer:

Lord, all of the money I have is from you. May I never allow it to take your place and become my god. Help me to teach my children how to handle money. Make me a good example as I learn to save, give, and spend wisely. Amen.

Activities:

Day 1 – Develop a plan to teach your children how to save, give, and spend wisely.

Day 2 – Create a chore chart. Even if your children are still babies, this will help prepare you for the years to come. An online program you might want to check out is www.myjobchart.com. This free program allows you to assign chores to each of your children, help them complete their jobs, and then help them divide their money into savings, spending, and giving.

Day 3 – Determine what chores you want to be mandatory and unpaid and what chores you want to be commission-based. Make a list of both. If your children are old enough, talk with them about their new responsibilities.

Day 4 – Are you setting a good example with your own spending, saving, and giving? Are there any changes you need to make? (I mentioned it earlier, but I'm reminding you again. Have you checked out Appendix C for more money-saving tips or my website for a free ebook, *Financial Freedom on a Fixed Income*?)

Day 5 – I've mentioned Dave Ramsey's website before. He has more information on how to teach your kids about money. Check it out: www.daveramsey.com.

WEEK 36:
LESSONS IN PROVERBS

Whoever fears the LORD has a secure fortress,
and for their children it will be a refuge.
Proverbs 14:26

We took my oldest son to the beach right after his first birthday. Unfortunately, the trip didn't go quite as well as I had hoped. The crash of the waves scared him, and the salt water (that he refused to stop tasting) made him cringe. Our trip would have been a disaster if not for the sand. He loved playing in it. We built a sandcastle, and he laughed with delight as we added each new element.

For some reason, most children love building sandcastles. I think maybe it's because they can imagine themselves living in them. Inside, they are kings and queens of the castle, safe from waves and intruders and protected with high walls.

Kids have the same kind of intrigue with forts. When it snows outside, my boys love to run from one fort to another in a snowball fight. When it rains, they can't wait to pull out a couple of chairs and a blanket and build an indoor fort. When I was growing up, we built huge forts in our living room and played in them for hours. Sometimes we ate lunch or even did our homework in them. There's just something special about being within a fort or sandcastle, especially one you built with your own hands.

Unfortunately, as kids grow older, their excitement fades. The day-to-day tasks of life squelch the carefree days of castle and fort building. Our kids quit creating safe havens, and if they're not careful, worry creeps into their lives. However, as parents, we can help.

Proverbs 14:26 says when we fear the Lord, we create a refuge for our children—a place for them to feel safe and secure. It makes sense, doesn't it? When we trust the Lord through our struggles, and our children see Him come through for us, they will be more likely to trust Him when they face a trial.

Hopefully, when they are too mature to build forts and too old to play in the sand, they will reside in the fortress of the Lord and rest their heads on the shoulder of the King.

Questions for Reflection:

1. How does it benefit your children when you trust the Lord?

2. How might it hinder their spiritual walk if you don't trust Him?

3. Why do you sometimes lack trust? Please be specific.

4. Describe an instance in which God came through for you.

5. In what other things (instead of God) might you be tempted to place your trust?

Prayer:

Father, you alone are strong enough to carry my worries, pains, and fears. No other refuge is good enough. Though I might try to lean on my family, my friends, or even myself, none of these will suffice. Only you can make me secure. May I trust in you so my children learn you are a safe place to rest. Amen.

Activities:

Day 1 – Build an indoor fort with your kids. Even if your children are too young to help, they will enjoy the time spent with you.

Day 2 – Tell your kids about a time when God was faithful to you.

Day 3 – Rest in God's protection today. Take at least thirty minutes to relax in the middle of the day.

Day 4 – Talk to another mother about your doubts and worries.

Day 5 – If you have access to a sandbox, build a sandcastle with your children.

WEEK 37:
LESSONS IN PROVERBS

Start children off on the way they should go, and even when they are old they will not turn from it. Proverbs 22:6

I have a friend who is a faithful disciple of Jesus. She works for a Christian organization and attends church on a regular basis. Her love for Jesus is obvious to those around her. Nonetheless, her son is an agnostic who turned his back on the Lord during his teen years. According to some, his lack of faith reflects her parenting. These people would (mistakenly) claim she didn't train him well. They might even use today's verse as "evidence." What these people fail to realize, though, is that they have taken this verse completely out of context.

Sometimes we feel it's our duty to share a biblical truth with another believer. We have the best of intentions, but unfortunately, we sometimes do more damage than good.

One such example is when we pull a verse like this one out of context and teach something God never intended us to teach.

Proverbs 22:6 says, *Start children off on the way they should go, and even when they are old they will not turn from it.* Some well-intentioned teachers have mistakenly taught this verse as a guarantee. If we teach our children correctly, they will never turn their backs on God. Many parents have felt beaten into the ground by well-meaning believers who teach about this verse.

However, God never intended for this to be a guarantee. The Proverbs are generalities. Generally, if we raise our children to know the Lord, they won't turn from it and will instead follow the path we lay for them. But not always. Sometimes a parent can do everything right and still have a child turn his back on the Lord. Rather than preach at parents who probably already feel like failures, we should encourage them. Their children's rebellion does not reflect their parenting ability.

On the other hand, because this proverb is generally true, we should take our job as parents seriously. What we do matters. When we feel like all we ever do is clean messes, deal with tantrums, and carpool to various activities, we must remind ourselves we are the primary influencers of young lives. Ruth Schwenk said it well in a blog post: "Sometimes it can be so easy to forget that we are raising the world-changers.[3]" No one influences children like their parents. As the saying goes, "Like father, like son. Like mother, like daughter."

Questions for Reflection:

1. Have any of your children turned their backs on the Lord? If so, pray for them today.

2. Why do you think children generally follow the path laid out by their parents?

3. What do you think causes some children to turn away from what their parents taught them?

4. How can you encourage someone who is struggling with a rebellious child? Please be specific.

Prayer:

Lord, you have given me an incredible task—to train my children to know and love you. I recognize I can't control their actions. They will ultimately do what they want to do. But guide me to do all I can to help them make wise choices. Amen.

Activities:

Day 1 – What can you do to help instill a love for the Lord in your children this week? List at least five specific ideas.

Day 2 –Think of someone you know whose child has turned away from God. Spend time in prayer for them today.

Day 3 – Send an encouraging email to the person you thought of on Day 2.

Day 4 – Sometimes, when kids won't listen to their

parents, they will listen to another caring adult. How can you mentor another child? Make a plan today to get involved in the youth group or children's ministry at church, join a local Boys and Girls Club, or find a neighbor child to mentor.

Day 5 – On Day 1, you listed five ideas to help instill a love for God in your children. Incorporate at least one of these ideas into your daily routine.

WEEK 38:
LESSONS IN PROVERBS

Discipline your children, and they will give you peace; they will bring you the delights you desire. Proverbs 29:17. See also Proverbs 13:24 and 22:15.

My dad loves to tell the story of our family trip to Yellowstone National Park. I don't remember the trip, but according to my parents, I had a rough time on the ride home, and my dad had to pull over and discipline me. I was a relatively obedient child, but when I threw a fit, I really threw one. For instance, when I was a toddler, I held my breath until I passed out because my older brother wouldn't give me a toy. Not just once, but several times, to my mother's horror.

On one hand, I hated when my parents disciplined me. After all, it's no fun to lose a privilege or get spanked. But on the other hand, I'm glad my parents were wise enough to recognize the value of discipline. Discipline, as painful as it may be for a parent to perform, and for the child to receive, is both necessary and beneficial. Our verse for today from Proverbs makes this clear: *Discipline your children, and they will give you peace.* I think the opposite is also true: don't discipline your child, and he will give you trouble.

The book of Proverbs explains the value of discipline over and over again. In Proverbs 22:15, the author writes, *Folly is bound up in the heart of a child, but the rod of discipline will drive it far away.* And again in Proverbs 13:24: *Whoever spares the rod hates their children, but the one who loves their children is careful to discipline them.* That's strong language. The parent who won't discipline *hates* his son.

It makes sense, though. When we fail to discipline our children, we set them up for failure. The working world won't allow them to do whatever they want without consequences. Neither will the law. If they don't learn to obey rules at home, where will they learn? We certainly don't want them to land in prison, in a failed marriage, or at rock bottom.

I'm the first to admit the difficulties of discipline. Discipline is difficult for a number of reasons. First of all, it's hard because it breaks our hearts to make our children cry. Last night, one of my sons refused to pick up his toys, so I sat him on his time-out rug. His poor little body shook as the sobs came. I was tempted to clean up the mess myself, give him a big hug, and forget that he ignored my request. But what would that teach him? As much as it hurt me, I stood my ground. And he learned. After his time-out, he picked up his toys—every single one of them.

Discipline is also difficult because there are so many conflicting opinions. While one expert claims you should never spank, another claims it's necessary. One child expert advises you never use time-out, while another encourages it. Discipline is one of those things every parent must decide for herself. By all means, pray and consult other parents and experts for advice. But then do what your heart tells you the right thing is to do. Trust the Holy Spirit within you, and refuse to allow another person's opinion to distract you from doing what you know you need to do.

Hebrews 12:6 says, *The Lord disciplines the one he loves, and he chastens everyone he accepts as a son.* God is our example, and He disciplines us because He loves us. I can think of no better example to follow.

Questions for Reflection:

1. What do you think about spanking? Spend some time discussing this with your spouse, if you're married.

2. How did your parents discipline you? What did they do well? What will you do differently?

3. Why is discipline necessary?

Prayer:

Father, just as you discipline us, you have commanded me to discipline my children. Not out of anger, but out of love. Give me wisdom in this difficult task. May I never go too far in anger, but always discipline in love. Amen.

Activities:

Day 1 – Check out Dr. Kevin Leman's book, *Making Children Mind Without Losing Yours* (Revell, 1984, 2000). It provides helpful tips to encourage obedience in your children.

Day 2 – Sometimes we have to choose our battles. Author and speaker Chip Ingram once said something along these lines: "You don't have to win every battle, but you want to win the war." What are some of the battles you are willing to give up? On the other hand, what are the non-negotiables in your family?

Day 3 – Research various discipline strategies this week.

Day 4 – Talk with your spouse (if you're married) about his views on discipline.

Day 5 – How has the Lord disciplined you? List a few specific examples.

Week 39:
The Ancestors of Jesus

This is the genealogy of Jesus the Messiah the son of David, the son of Abraham. Matthew 1:1

I thought I knew about parenting. Then I had kids. Before having a child of my own, I thought things like this:

I'll never do that with my child.

I'm not going to let my infant control my life like that mother does.

I'm going to nurse for at least a year.

I would never allow my toddler to act that way in public.

How my thoughts changed when I actually had children! All of my so-called knowledge disappeared. Instead of feeling confident, I felt unqualified and wondered why God trusted me with this tiny, helpless baby. Someone else could surely do a better job, someone who was smarter or more patient or more loving than me.

But God doesn't always use the most likely person for

the job. In fact, sometimes He uses the least likely. For instance, David was a murderer, Tamar slept with her father-in-law, Rahab was a prostitute, Ruth was a young widow, Bathsheba cheated on her husband, Manasseh was the most evil king of Judah, and Mary was pregnant out of wedlock. Each of these was an ancestor of Jesus listed in Matthew chapter one. God could have done it some other way, but He chose to use broken, sinful people to bring His Son into the world. He designed it in such a way that Jesus Christ, God in the flesh, came from unqualified people.

So it is with us. God didn't have to design parenthood like He did. He could have developed some other way to continue the population. Instead, He chose to use us, unqualified as we may be, to raise our children to know and love Him. On days when our children are fussy, the house is a mess, and we're exhausted, it's helpful to remember that God desired us. Despite our flaws, despite our inadequacies, despite our sins, He picked us. He chose us to be His hands and feet to the ones who call us Mommy.

Questions for Reflection:

1. In what areas of your life do you feel inadequate?

2. How could God use your inadequacies for His glory?

3. Why do you think God chooses broken, sinful people to accomplish His plan?

4. What is your greatest weakness when it comes to parenting?

5. What is your greatest strength?

Prayer:

Lord, you are aware of all my inadequacies—my flaws, my sins, and my failures. You still chose me for the important job of raising children to know and serve you. When I feel unqualified, remind me of that truth. And when I fail, use me anyway, in spite of my flaws. Amen.

Activities:

Day 1 – In question one, you listed areas in which you feel inadequate. Spend time in prayer over these areas today.

Day 2 – Look in your Bible at the stories of some of the unlikely people God used:
-Jacob (His story begins in Genesis 25.)
-Rahab (You first read about her in Joshua 2.)
-Ruth (You can read about her in the book of Ruth.)
-Bathsheba (Look at 2 Samuel 11 for her story.)

Day 3 – In question four, you described your greatest weakness. What can you do to improve this area of your life? Do it today.

Day 4 – How can you be the hands and feet of Jesus to your children? List at least five ways.

Day 5 – On day four, you listed five ways to be the hands and feet of Jesus. Choose at least one of these ideas to do today.

WEEK 40:
MARY, PART 1

"I am the Lord's servant," Mary answered. "May your word to me be fulfilled." Then the angel left her. Luke 1:38

A friend of mine (we'll call her Melissa) bought a pregnancy test and a bottle of wine. After all, she was certain she wasn't pregnant and planned to celebrate with her husband once the test read negative. Imagine her surprise when she saw two lines instead of one. There was no celebration that night. Instead of tears of joy, she cried tears of disappointment. Don't get me wrong. Once the pregnancy progressed, her disappointment changed to excitement. She eventually accepted God's plan for her life. But it was hard. It wasn't what she planned. It wasn't what she originally wanted. She had a three-month-old baby at home and didn't feel ready to do it all over again.

I imagine Mary experienced some of the same feelings

my friend did. Mary was young, in love, and planning her wedding when the angel broke the news to her: *But the angel said to her, "Do not be afraid, Mary; you have found favor with God. You will conceive and give birth to a son, and you are to call him Jesus. He will be great and will be called the Son of the Most High. The Lord God will give him the throne of his father David"* (Luke 1:30-32).

If I were she, I think I would have questioned the angel a little bit more. "Could we wait until after I get married? Am I the best person for the job? Are you sure? Didn't you say I found favor with God? Why would He do this to me if I found favor with Him?" But Mary didn't ask these questions. When the angel shattered all her plans, she replied, "*May your word to me be fulfilled.*" She accepted God's plan, even though it wasn't what she wanted. She, of course, didn't want people to gossip about her, didn't want to ruin her reputation, and certainly didn't want to risk losing the person she loved. But when Mary faced all these trials, she accepted them as God's plan for her life. That's probably one of the reasons God chose her: she was willing to follow His plan regardless of the difficulties that came with it.

As we parent our children, God might change our plans just like He changed Mary's plans and just like He changed my friend's plans. He might bring another child into our lives when we don't think we want another one. He might lead us to move our family somewhere we don't want to go. He might ask us to change jobs, consider foster care, or think about adoption.

Each of these decisions doesn't just affect us; it affects

our children as well. It's one thing to do something we don't want to do; it's even more difficult to do something our kids don't want us to do. But, as Mary's story teaches us, it's worth it if God is in charge. If He's the one leading us, it's worth it to say, "May your word to me be fulfilled." With Mary, these words resulted in the King of the Universe being born. Who knows what will happen when we utter them?

Questions for Reflection:

1. How do you think Mary felt when the angel told her the news? Please be specific.

2. How would you have reacted if you had been Mary?

3. What are some other biblical examples of God changing someone's plans?

4. Has God ever changed your plans? If so, please describe.

5. What do your children learn when you accept God's plan for your life?

Prayer:

Lord, you are in charge. Your plans are bigger and better than mine, and you know what's best for my family. Sometimes it's difficult to accept your plan for my life, especially when it's different than my own plan. Change my heart and make it moldable like Mary's. Amen.

Activities:

Day 1 – Memorize Jeremiah 29:11.

Day 2 – What are your plans for this year? Write them.

Day 3 – What are your plans for the next five years? Write these as well.

Day 4 – There's nothing wrong with having plans, as long as we are willing to change them if God asks us to. Pray about the plans you wrote in Days Two and Three.

Day 5 – If your children are old enough, play a game of "Red Light, Green Light" with them. Go when the leader says, "Green Light," and stop when he says, "Red Light." Use this game to explain to your children that we go when God tells us to go, and we stop when He tells us to stop.

WEEK 41:
MARY, PART 2

Near the cross of Jesus stood his mother ...
John 19:25

Audrey was seven years old when diagnosed with leukemia. In the midst of chemotherapy, fevers, and infections, there was at least one bright spot in her life: the shaving party. Rather than watch their daughter suffer alone as her hair fell out, her parents, Eric and Sharon, threw a shaving party and allowed their children to shave their heads. Audrey would not be the only one without hair in their family. Though they could have felt helpless, they instead chose to do what they could. They couldn't take away her pain, and they couldn't promise healing. What they could do was turn a sad moment into a treasured memory.

Mary, the mother of Jesus, was a lot like Eric and Sharon in this respect. She was raising the Son of God, after all, so

I'm sure she felt overwhelmed and helpless at times. I'm sure she questioned herself and wondered if there was anything she could do to encourage her Son. How do you encourage God anyway? One time I'm certain she felt helpless was while Jesus—the child she raised from infancy—hung on the cross to die. Mary could have wallowed in self-pity, but instead, she did what she could and stood by her beloved Son until the end.

When the majority of Jesus' disciples turned their backs on Him and fled, she stayed near. When the leaders of the town mocked Him, she remained loyal. When most of the townspeople thought He was insane or evil, she refused to believe the lies. She believed in her Son until the end. It was all she could do, but I imagine it meant the world to Jesus.

There will be times in which we feel helpless too. When our child becomes sick, doesn't make the baseball team, or gets her heart broken, we will want to help but wonder how. In those moments, we will have a choice: to give in to the helplessness and self-pity, or do what we can and be there for them. We might not be able to fix the problem. We might not be able to stop their tears. But we can offer a shoulder to cry on. Maybe, like Eric and Sharon, we can turn a devastating moment into a treasured memory.

Questions for Reflection:

1. When have you felt helpless as a parent?

2.   What causes your children to hurt? Please be specific.

3.   Along with being there for your children when they are hurting, what are some other practical ways you can encourage them when they hurt?

Prayer:

Father, you know what it's like to watch a child suffer. You experienced it when Jesus died on the cross. You watched Him hurt and heard Him cry. Help us to encourage our children when they hurt. Give us wisdom to know what to say to them and when to not say anything. Let them feel our love, even in the midst of their pain. Amen.

Activities:

Day 1 – Practice being present with your children this week. Today, watch their favorite movie or television show with them.

Day 2 – Go on a walk with your kids.

Day 3 – Ask your children questions. Some sample questions include: What is your favorite animal? Of what are you afraid? What is your favorite color? What is your favorite food? What's your favorite Bible story?

Day 4 – Do an art project with your kids today.

Day 5 – Spend at least thirty minutes with each child. Don't think about anything else or multi-task. Instead, give each of them one hundred percent of your attention.

WEEK 42:
MARY AND JOSEPH

When Joseph and Mary had done everything required by the Law of the Lord, they returned to Galilee to their own town of Nazareth.
Luke 2:39

My tongue needs the most taming when I'm driving. It's the one situation in which I seem to get frustrated easily. If someone pulls out in front of my car, neglects to use a turn signal, or doesn't seem to understand the speed limit is not fifteen miles per hour on the highway, I am tempted to utter unkind words. Not to them, of course, but aloud nonetheless, and often within the presence of moldable ears.

I'm also tempted to speed. I assume many parents can understand. I'm ready on time, but then my son has a blowout in his diaper. Or, maybe he decides to vomit all over the front of my shirt. Some childhood crisis always seems to put us behind schedule. So again, I have a choice in my vehicle: be a good example by obeying the law, even if I arrive late, or choose to break the law to get there on time.

Someone without children might be tempted to think, "Why don't you just get up earlier? Then you wouldn't have to face such a tough decision." But anyone with children knows that no matter how early we get up, something can still interrupt the routine. We will run late at some point or another and be tempted to break the speed limit to arrive on time.

We might think speeding is no big deal or assume everyone goes a few miles over. But what does that teach our children? That it's okay to break the law a little bit? That it's okay to sin, as long as it's just a little sin?

Instead, we should follow the example of Joseph and Mary. They circumcised Jesus on the eighth day, followed the purification rituals, and presented Jesus at the Temple at the appropriate time. They did *everything required by the Law*. No exceptions. They didn't make excuses for disobedience.

By their example, they taught their children it's not okay to break the law, not even a little bit. For Joseph and Mary, obedience was a lifestyle. It was who they were. Can the same be said of me? I wish it could, but in my vehicle at least, it probably can't.

Questions for Reflection:

1. In what circumstances are you tempted to break the law? (Either God's law or the law of the land.)

2. Is it ever okay to break the law? If so, when?

3. How does your obedience, or lack of obedience, affect your children?

Prayer:

God, you desire obedience. In fact, you command it. Don't allow me to become desensitized to sin. Instead, make my heart break because of disobedience. Lord, help me to choose obedience when I am tempted to sin. Amen.

Activities:

Day 1 – In your vehicle today, take mental note of your actions, words, and thoughts. How often do you speed? How often do unkind words slip from your tongue?

Day 2 – What other place is a hotspot for temptation? Try to determine when and where you are most tempted to sin.

Day 3 – Talk to your children about obeying the law.

Day 4 – Create consequences for yourself for giving in to temptation. For example, no dessert if you speed this week, etc.

Day 5 – Choose a role model for obedience, and follow the example of this person.

WEEK 43:
ZECHARIAH AND ELIZABETH

Both of them were righteous in the sight of God, observing all the Lord's commands and decrees blamelessly. But they were childless, because Elizabeth was not able to conceive, and they were both very old. Luke 1:6-7

Every month, we bought a pregnancy test. Every month, the test read negative. And every month, we were disappointed. Trying to get pregnant is emotionally exhausting when it doesn't happen as soon as we would like. We wonder if something is wrong with us, we wonder why it's not happening, and we question if it's ever going to happen.

Imagine how Zechariah and Elizabeth must have felt. Month after month, year after year, decade after decade, and still no children. Plus, in their culture, not being able to conceive was viewed as a curse from God. Not only did they have to deal with their own feelings of disappointment, they also had to deal with their friends' and neighbors' judgment. Even in the midst of their frustrations, they continued to pray and wait for the Lord.

I wonder if I would have been so patient. Whether it is a long line at the grocery store, a traffic jam, crowds at an amusement park, or unanswered prayer, I struggle to wait. Below are a few tips that have helped me practice the discipline of waiting:

1. Develop a prayer journal (like the one we talked about in Week 33). On the left side of a sheet of paper, make columns for the date and for the prayer request. Then, on the right side of the paper, make another column for the date on which God answered the prayer, as well as a description of how He answered it. Keep in mind the answer might be "no." This will help you see God is answering your prayers, even if not in the way you would like.

2. Don't put too many activities or tasks on your to-do list or daily planner. Try to spread your chores throughout the week. For instance, plan to do laundry on Monday, grocery shopping on Tuesday, cleaning on Wednesday, budgeting on Thursday, etc. This will help you not stress when things take longer than expected.

3. Choose the slow line at the grocery store sometimes. Nothing better than practice, right?

4. Bring a book or magazine to read while you wait for an appointment. This will help the wait time

go faster. Plus, you'll get to read, something many parents never find time to do.

5. Observe a day of rest. It doesn't have to be Sunday, but it needs to happen. Choose a day each week to rest and refocus on the Lord.

Zechariah and Elizabeth weren't without flaws. When God finally told them they would have a baby, they doubted. Zechariah asked the angel God sent, "*How can I be sure of this? I am an old man and my wife is well along in years*" (Luke 1:18). They clearly weren't perfect. But to their credit, they waited well—much better than I probably would have.

Questions for Reflection:

1. Which of the above tips would you like to put into practice?

2. Why is waiting for the Lord so difficult?

3. Why do you think God sometimes seems slow in answering prayers?

Prayer:

Lord, give me patience, especially when I'm waiting on you. Help me trust that you are listening and will answer. Your answer might not be what I want or what I think is best, but I recognize your plans are bigger than mine. Mold my heart to accept those difficult answers. Amen.

Activities:

Day 1 – Make a prayer journal as described in the first tip.

Day 2 – Evaluate your daily planner or calendar. Make any necessary changes.

Day 3 – With your children, create a prayer wall. Record prayer requests and answers to prayers. Hang this somewhere in your home as a reminder that God does answer prayer.

Day 4 – Search the Bible for other people who had to wait on God. Some people you might want to read about include: Joseph, Moses, David, and Paul. Each of these biblical figures learned to wait on God.

Day 5 – Observe a day of rest with your family.

WEEK 44:
ZEBEDEE

And immediately they left the boat and their father and followed him. Matthew 4:22. See also Mark 1:19-20.

My dad doesn't cry often, but at my wedding, as he walked me down the aisle, I saw tears form in his eyes. I've never asked him why he cried, but I have a pretty good guess. He was letting me go, entrusting me into another man's hands. And now that I'm a parent, I understand how difficult it is to let a child go.

Unfortunately, there's no avoiding it. We let go a little bit when our child takes his first step and again when he rides his first bike. We experience that inner turmoil as we send our child off to school for the first time or hesitantly hand over the car keys. I don't even want to think about high school graduation and college.

Letting go is difficult, plain and simple, but it is the

destiny of every parent. Parenting has never been about keeping our children close to us. It's about preparing them to leave, raising them to be men and women who will go into the world and make a difference.

Zebedee understood this well. He and his two sons, James and John, were fisherman. One day, they were on the Sea of Galilee, preparing their fishing nets and hoping to get a large catch for all their hard work when Jesus called to James and John from the shore. The brothers left their father to follow Jesus. They didn't finish their work, didn't help bring the boat back to shore, and didn't help with the nets. They followed immediately.

If I were Zebedee, I think I would have been a bit irritated. I probably would have complained, "At least let them help me dock the boat, Jesus. After all, I'm already out here, and I really need a good catch to help me pay this month's bills. Can't they come to you later, after we've finished working today?" Zebedee, though, didn't say a word.

He must have understood the bigger picture—that it's not about preserving our kids, but preparing them to go wherever God leads them. Sometimes, God might lead them halfway across the world or into a profession we might not understand. As much as we'd love to always have our children and grandchildren near, that might not be God's plan for their lives. The question is, will we be okay with God's plan even if it's different than ours? Zebedee was, but sometimes I wonder about myself.

Questions for Reflection:

1. When have you experienced that "letting go" feeling? Why is letting go so difficult?

2. What can you do to better prepare your children for life on their own?

3. How would you react if Jesus called your children to move away from you?

Prayer:

Father, you are the ultimate example of letting go. It must have been devastating to watch Jesus come to earth, knowing what we would do to Him. But you recognized it was necessary and did it willingly. Help me to remember my goal as a parent—to raise children who follow you wherever you lead. Amen.

Activities:

Day 1 – If your children are old enough, plan a sleepover with one of their friends.

Day 2 – Write a paragraph about what it means to "let go" of your children.

Day 3 – If you're married, plan to have a date night at least once a month. Write this month's date on the calendar. Eventually, your kids will be gone. Make sure you and your spouse still love each other when that day comes.

Day 4 – Write a letter to your child's future spouse.

Day 5 – If your parents or in-laws live near you, visit
them this weekend.

WEEK 45:
ZEBEDEE'S WIFE

Then the mother of Zebedee's sons came to Jesus with her sons and, kneeling down, asked a favor of him. "What is it you want?" he asked. She said, "Grant that one of these two sons of mine may sit at your right and the other at your left in your kingdom." Matthew 20:20-21

It's easy to make life all about us and our families, especially in those early years when our days and nights fade together. As moms, we feel like we are serving all the time (and, truth be told, we are!) so we sometimes don't want to serve anyone else in our down time. We'd much rather rest or do something we want to do for a change.

The problem with this, though, is that if our kids never see us serve anyone outside our family, from whom will they learn to serve? The truth is, they won't learn.

A friend of mine is a great example of someone who serves,

both within and outside of her family. We'll call her Sarah and her husband Derek. A couple of years ago, Derek and Sarah learned about a teenage girl in the area who was struggling at home. They wanted to help her by offering a place to stay, but there were several factors stopping them. First, money was tight as a family of four on one income. Could they afford to take care of another child? Plus, their house wasn't large. With three bedrooms, the only way they could provide a room for this young woman was by asking their two boys to share a room. And what would they do if they decided to have another child? They didn't know how it would work, but they had to try. They were compelled to serve. Disregarding difficulties, they moved her into their home.

Contrast my friends Derek and Sarah with Zebedee's wife. Derek and Sarah put their family's needs aside to serve someone else. Zebedee's wife sought for her children to be served. She came to Jesus and begged him, "*Grant that one of these two sons of mine may sit at your right and the other at your left in your kingdom.*" She wanted her kids, James and John, to be first in line, right behind Jesus.

It's easy to understand why. She loved her children and wanted them to succeed. What parent doesn't want that for her children? The aspirations to succeed aren't wrong in themselves as long as we're also teaching our kids to serve and not focusing so much on success that they miss the bigger picture. After all, it is through service that our children reach their full potential. Jesus said that w*hoever wants to become great among you must be your servant, and whoever wants to be first must be your slave* (Matthew 20:26-27).

My friend's children will likely be two of the great people Jesus talked about. After all, they're learning early to put their own desires aside for the benefit of others. Granted, they might not remember much about this time in their lives. But I think they'll remember enough. They'll remember how their parents taught them to serve. They'll remember how good it felt to help someone else. Imagine the difference they'll make in the years to come.

I think Zebedee's wife also learned this lesson. It may have taken her awhile, but she did eventually learn to serve. I say this because of what she did when Jesus died. Instead of running away as most of His followers did, she stayed at the cross, serving Him in the only way she could. She wasn't asking for her sons to be first in line anymore. Now all she wanted was to help her Lord and Savior, Jesus Christ.

Questions for Reflection:

1. How can you teach your children the importance of service?

2. What makes service difficult for you? How can you overcome these difficulties?

3. How can you serve your children this week?

Prayer:

Lord, you called me to service—to put you first, others second, and myself last. Don't allow my pride to get in the way of service. Instead, give me humility and a servant's heart. May I follow the example of Jesus in all I do. In doing so, I want to teach my children to serve as well. Amen.

Activities:

Brainstorm ways to serve the following people. Plan to serve each group at least once over the next month:

Day 1 – Your Family

Day 2 – Your Friends

Day 3 – Your Church Family

Day 4 – Your Neighbors

Day 5 – A Local Ministry

WEEK 46:
JAIRUS

Then one of the synagogue leaders, named Jairus, came, and when he saw Jesus, he fell at his feet. He pleaded earnestly with him, "My little daughter is dying. Please come and put your hands on her so that she will be healed and live." Mark 5:22-23. See also Matthew 9 and Luke 8.

My oldest son, Rylan, got his first black eye yesterday. He was chasing one of his friends around the living room, tripped over a toy, and planted his cheekbone right into the corner of our coffee table. My reaction? I wish I could say I immediately went to the Lord and taught my son the importance of bringing our hurts to the Healer, but unfortunately, I didn't. My first reaction was to call the doctor to see how to minimize the swelling and discoloration.

Don't get me wrong. I believe in medical care, and I

believe in seeking the wisdom of those who have dedicated their lives to helping others. But, I also believe in the power of prayer. *That* is where we should turn first. Granted, it might be a quick prayer as we dial 911 or jump in the minivan to head to the emergency room, but it shouldn't be a last resort.

Parent after parent in the Bible makes this clear. Jairus is one example. He brought his dying daughter to Jesus and pled for healing. At first glance, this story doesn't seem that incredible. Lots of parents brought their sick children to God, but Jairus was a ruler of the synagogue. That means he would have been in close contact with many Pharisees. For him to fall at the feet of Jesus and plead for help was not only humbling, but also risky. The Pharisees hated Jesus. They plotted His death and wanted nothing more than to quiet this preacher (and any of His followers) who threatened their positions.

Jairus didn't care. Regardless of who was watching and what they might think, he brought his daughter to the only One who could save her. This story is retold in Matthew 9 and Luke 8. Look at what Jairus said in Matthew 9:18: *Put your hand on her, and **she will live*** (emphasis mine).

Sometimes when we come before the Lord, we lack this kind of faith. Instead of "she will live," we tend to think, "she might live." How easily we forget Jesus has been there. He experienced pain like few of us can even imagine, but He also conquered it. Jesus didn't remain dead. He healed Himself. Who better to bring our children to than the One who was able to heal Himself from death?

By all means, take advantage of the medical professionals God has given you. But don't forget about the One who is able to heal when all else can't, the One who said to us, *Come to me, all you who are weary and burdened, and I will give you rest* (Matthew 11:28).

Questions for Reflection:

1. Describe an instance in which your children have been sick or hurt. What was your reaction? How long was it before you came to the Lord in prayer?

2. Other than God, who else can you rely on in a crisis?

3. Why does God sometimes not heal our loved ones, even when we come to Him first?

Prayer:

My God and my Healer, create more faith within me so I turn to you first—not after I've tried everything else, but before I've tried anything. I know you are able to heal any ailment that might come my way. Help me to remember that in the midst of a crisis and turn to you first. Amen.

Activities:

Day 1 – In an earlier devotion, you memorized Matthew 11:28. Do you still know it? If not, work on it again.

Day 2 – Read in Matthew 17 and Mark 9 about other children whom Jesus healed.

Day 3 – Make an emergency contact form to post on your refrigerator. Prayer is important, but so is preparedness.

Day 4 – Create a first aid kit with your children. Talk to them about how God sometimes uses medicine to help heal our bodies.

Day 5 – With your children, create a list of prayer needs. Add these prayer needs to the prayer wall you made in Week 43.

Week 47:
Widow

When the Lord saw her, his heart went out to her and he said, "Don't cry." Luke 7:13

For some reason, kids always seem to get sick when the doctors are unavailable—either on a weekend or right after they close for the day. My oldest son's first fever hit on a Friday night when he was a little over a month old. As a new parent, I had no idea what to do, and my husband and parents were out of town. I called the nurse hotline number my pediatrician had given me, and she asked me to take his temperature. She wanted me to call her back once I took it. (I don't know if you've ever tried to take the temperature of a screaming, squirming newborn, but let me tell you, it's not as simple as it sounds—especially for a new mom.) Thirty minutes later, the nurse called me back. Between sobs, I explained I couldn't get Rylan to stop crying and squirming long enough to get an accurate reading.

Sometimes, I wonder what the Lord is doing when we're upset. When we're crying at two o'clock in the morning because we can't get our two-week-old baby to eat, when we're lying on our child's hospital bed, when we break down at the end of a long day, I wonder what God is doing. I've heard people say He's carrying us through these times, but I think He's also crying with us. I think He's peering down at us and weeping as we weep. I could be wrong, but based on how Jesus reacted with this widow, I don't think I am.

This woman had already lost her husband, and now her son was dead as well. She was broken when Jesus found her. *As he approached the town gate, a dead person was being carried out—the only son of his mother, and she was a widow. And a large crowd from the town was with her. When the Lord saw her, his heart went out to her and he said, "Don't cry"* (Luke 7:12-13). Jesus didn't have to stop for this woman. I imagine He was busy with other miracles to perform and other lessons to teach His disciples. He had a large crowd with Him, after all. Nonetheless, He noticed this woman, and His heart broke with hers. He didn't allow His agenda to keep Him from hurting with her.

Rest assured, His agenda won't keep Him from us either. When we are hurting, He'll notice. When our hearts are breaking, His will too. He might not fix the problem like He did for this widow, raising her dead son to life. He took away the woman's tears, but He might not always take away ours. Sometimes the tears continue to fall. But, there is something He will do, and it's vital we recognize it. He will be with us, He will cry with us, and He will make sure we never weep alone.

Questions for Reflection:

1. When have you felt alone?

2. Other than the Lord, whom can you turn to in times of pain?

3. God doesn't always fix a problem and take away the pain. Why?

4. Describe an instance in which you felt the Lord's presence with you during a difficult time.

5. Is there anything you can do to help you feel closer to the Lord during a difficult time? If so, please describe.

Prayer:

Father, as Jesus' heart went out to the widow in her time of pain, I believe your heart goes out to me as well. You are my rock. You are my refuge. Help me lean on you when I struggle. May I feel your presence when I'm broken and know you are there for me always. Amen.

Activities:

Day 1 – Tell a friend, spouse, or mentor what you have struggled with lately.

Day 2 – Draw a picture of a rainy day with your children. I like to think that when it rains, it's like God crying with someone in need.

Day 3 – If you have a friend who is hurting, cry with her today.

Day 4 – If you're going through a difficult time, check out Philip Yancey's books, *Where is God When It Hurts?* and *Disappointment with God.* Another great book is *Plan B: What Do You Do When God Doesn't Show Up the Way You Thought He Would?* by Pete Wilson.

Day 5 – Open your heart to the Lord and tell Him your hurts and frustrations. Don't hold anything back from Him.

Week 48:
Father in the Parable of the Prodigal Son

So he got up and went to his father. But while he was still a long way off, his father saw him and was filled with compassion for him; he ran to his son, threw his arms around him and kissed him. Luke 15:20

Sonny lost his battle with cancer at only 47 years old. He left behind a wife of 27 years, Tess, and two children in their early twenties. The night before Sonny's funeral, Tess complimented her father-in-law, Henry, sharing how he had been there every step of the way, not just for Sonny, but also for her.

"You have been the picture of God to me," she told him.

That's the job of a parent—to be the picture of God to his or her children. The father in the parable of the prodigal son did this well.

Rejected and humiliated, the father had every right to be upset with his son. By requesting his inheritance early, the son basically said, "I wish you were dead." In that culture, this was unforgivable. There was no turning back.

After wasting all of his father's money on his immoral lifestyle, the son hit rock bottom. He had no money, no job, and no food. *When he came to his senses, he said, "How many of my father's hired servants have food to spare, and here I am starving to death!"* (Luke 15:17). He decided to go home and thought maybe his father would at least treat him like a servant.

Much to his surprise, his father treated him *better* than a servant. When he arrived, his father didn't slap him across the face and disown him, though many of his neighbors would have expected it. He didn't even make him beg or lecture him on his poor choices. Not this father. Instead, he ran to his son, something men in his culture did not do. He didn't even wait for his son to apologize before he started planning the celebration. That is the picture of a great father—one who loves his children even when it hurts, one who welcomes them back regardless of how long they have been gone, and one who shows them what God is like.

Sonny was a father like this. He was a songwriter, and at his funeral, the preacher read the words to his final song:

He's a son's first hero
A daughter's first love
He's at home with a doll

And a baseball glove
He's teddy bear soft
And Superman tough
A son's first hero
A daughter's first love[4]

Sonny was a great father—not because of the money he spent on his kids or the things he did for them. He was a great father because he was their hero. He was their picture of God.

Questions for Reflection:

1. In what ways are parents visual representations of God?

2. How would you have reacted if you had been the father in this parable?

3. What makes a great parent? Please list a few characteristics.

Prayer:

Lord, use me in my children's lives. Help me to represent you well in everything I do. Help my children see your character in my life. When they look at me, I want them to see your face. Amen.

Activities:

Day 1 – List five specific ways you represent God to your
children.

Day 2 – What do you think God looks like? Draw a
picture of Him.

Day 3 – Now ask your children to draw a picture of
God. It's always fun to see how their little minds
picture things.

Day 4 – Spend time in the Word, getting to know your
Father better. The more you know Him, the
more you'll be like Him.

Day 5 – Memorize the fruit of the Spirit passage in
Galatians 5:22-23.

Week 49:
Parents of the Blind Man

*"We know he is our son," the parents
answered, "and we know he was born blind.
But how he can see now, or who opened his
eyes, we don't know. Ask him. He is of age; he
will speak for himself."* John 9:20-21

Caden, our youngest child, had taken a decent nap and eaten
a large snack, so I thought he would be fine at the grocery
store. I couldn't have been more wrong. He had meltdown
after meltdown and fit after fit. When he saw the bananas,
he cried for them. When he saw the animal crackers, again
he fussed. Nothing satisfied him.

I'd like to say I handled this particular meltdown with
grace, got him calmed down, and then received the "mother
of the year" award. But I didn't. To be honest, I wasn't even
thinking about what he needed and why he was fussy. I was
too worried about what other people were thinking of me as

a mother. I focused on the thoughts of people I didn't know rather than on the needs of my child.

In this instance, I was a lot like the parents of the blind man in John 9. Let's take a look at their story. Their son was born blind and lived his entire life without the gift of sight. One Sabbath day, Jesus healed him. The Pharisees, of course, were furious because Jesus healed the man on the Sabbath, the day that was supposed to be reserved for rest. The Pharisees questioned the man, but refused to believe his story.

They instead called for his parents to question them. *"Is this your son?" they asked. "Is this the one you say was born blind? How is it that now he can see?"*

"We know he is our son," the parents answered, "and we know he was born blind. But how he can see now, or who opened his eyes, we don't know. Ask him. He is of age" (John 9:19-21).

Jesus healed their son of a life-long ailment, but they were too afraid of the religious leaders to rejoice with their child. They didn't want to be criticized for believing in Jesus or kicked out of the synagogue as the Pharisees had previously threatened. So, rather than rejoice with their son, they kept their mouths shut and worried about what the religious leaders thought of them.

I used to be quick to judge the blind man's parents. After all, how selfish of them to ignore their son's healing and focus only on the leaders' opinions of them. Now though,

I understand their predicament. It's a temptation among many parents. Maybe it's in a playgroup where our child seems to be the only one acting up, at a grocery store where our child throws himself on the floor in a fit of rage, or at church where ours is the only inconsolable kid in nursery.

We worry about what other people think of us, as if their opinions determine our success or failure as parents. We exaggerate how long our babies sleep, downplay their fits, and most certainly don't allow anyone to see us reach our breaking points. Rather than focus our efforts on parenting to the best of our abilities, we focus our efforts on looking good. If only we would realize that we are all in this thing together. Let's stop comparing ourselves to one another and start helping each other instead.

Questions for Reflection:

1. On a scale of 1-10 (1 being not very much, 10 being a lot) how much do you focus on what others think of you?

2. Why do you worry about what others think of you?

3. What can you do to focus on God's opinion, rather than on other people's opinions?

Prayer:

Father, I want to please you. More than anyone else, I want you to be happy with me. When I fall into the trap of focusing on other people's opinions, especially as I parent the children you have given me, turn my mind back to you and your thoughts. Amen.

Activities:

Day 1 – Read Psalm 139 and Zephaniah 3:17. After looking at these verses, write down what God thinks of you.

Day 2 – Pay attention to your thoughts today. Do you find yourself focusing on what other people think of you or on what God thinks of you?

Day 3 – Write a letter to yourself about why you don't want to focus on the opinions of other people.

Day 4 – Tell a struggling mother she is doing a good job.

Day 5 – Spend time cuddling with your children today.

WEEK 50:
EUNICE

I am reminded of your sincere faith, which first lived in your grandmother Lois and in your mother Eunice and, I am persuaded, now lives in you also. 2 Timothy 1:5

Paul was an Israelite among Israelites, the greatest missionary who ever lived, and the writer of much of the New Testament. When looking for someone to mentor, Timothy was not Paul's most logical choice. Timothy was young, inexperienced, and timid. His mother was a believer, but as far as we know, his father was not (Acts 16:1). Nonetheless, Paul chose him. Timothy went on to lead an important church in Ephesus and lived each day as a minister of the Gospel.

Eunice must have been proud because it was her influence that brought her son to the Lord. Paul told Timothy in 2 Timothy 1:5, *I am reminded of your sincere faith, which first lived in your grandmother Lois and in your mother Eunice and, I am persuaded, now lives in you also.*

I wish we knew what Eunice did to lead her son to love Jesus. Did she say something in particular? Or maybe she did something special? What parenting style did she follow? How did she discipline?

I'm one of those people who loves formulas. A plus B equals C. You tell me the steps I need to take to be a good mom, and I'll follow your advice. The Bible, though, doesn't ever give us a formula for parenting. When I first became a mom, this was discouraging. I wanted a formula. I *needed* a formula. I'm learning, though, that not having a formula is a good thing. God gave us something even better. He gave us freedom—freedom to be the moms He designed us to be. All he asks is that we follow after Him as we parent.

We don't know what Eunice did to raise such a godly young man, but I can promise you one thing: she followed the Lord in everything she did. I imagine if she had a life verse, it might have been Colossians 3:17: *And whatever you do, whether in word or deed, do it all in the name of the Lord Jesus, giving thanks to God the Father through him.* Even though her husband didn't support her belief in Jesus, she was still faithful.

In her words and in her actions, Eunice showed Timothy what it meant to love Jesus. Years later, when Timothy was old enough to choose for himself to follow Jesus, he chose to be like his mother, not his unbelieving father.

Some Christians don't have believing spouses, and some are unwed. In these situations, living as a faithful believer is more difficult but not impossible. Having an unbelieving spouse or no spouse at all is no excuse to neglect your child's relationship with Jesus. Of course we'll make mistakes, and we'll lose our temper at times. Nonetheless, our kids should see a difference in us. When we fail, they should see us apologize. When we hurt, they should see us come to the Lord. When we talk to our neighbors or coworkers, they should see our love for Jesus. They are watching. The question is, what do they see today?

Questions for Reflection:

1. If you do not have a believing spouse (or are unmarried), what is most difficult about being the primary one to raise your child to know the Lord?

2. What are some practical ways to teach your children about the Lord?

3. Who most influenced you in your decision to follow Jesus? What did this person do?

Prayer:

Lord, you have given me a huge responsibility to raise my children to know you. Sometimes I don't know what to do. I feel so unqualified. But God, I know you can enable me. Guide me. Help me live Colossians 3:17 every day. Amen.

Activities:

Day 1 – Memorize Colossians 3:17 with your children.

Day 2 – In Week 48, you memorized Galatians 5:22-23. Which fruits of the Spirit do you struggle with most and why?

Day 3 – Color a tree with your children. Draw each of the fruits of the Spirit on the tree.

Day 4 – Talk with your children this week about why you chose to give your life to Jesus. If you haven't yet made this decision and are interested in learning more about it, contact your local church or shoot me an email for more information. (You can contact me through my website, www.lindseymbell.com).

Day 5 – In question three, you shared who influenced you most in your relationship with Jesus. Thank this person for his or her investment.

WEEK 51:
THE JAILER AND THE
CHRISTIANS AT TYRE

*The jailer brought them into his house and
set a meal before them; he was filled with joy
because he had come to believe in God—he
and his whole household.* Acts 16:34

*When it was time to leave, we left and
continued on our way. All of them, including
wives and children, accompanied us out of the
city, and there on the beach we knelt to pray.*
Acts 21:5

Every spring and fall, our church plans a Great Day of
Service. On these days, families go into the community and
help individuals who are unable to do lawn work or home
improvements. This year, I went to a home where we moved

rocks and built a wheelchair ramp—a lot of heavy lifting and work with power tools. It was not the ideal place for children, some might think. After all, there's not much for them to do anyway, and their presence might slow the work.

In truth, the children probably did slow the work because they weren't able to help with much. Nonetheless, they did what they could. One young girl planted flowers, and another moved small rocks from a large pile to a pickup truck. They might not have done a lot, but I'm glad they were there, because, where else could they learn about getting dirty for the Lord? Where else could they learn to serve?

I think the jailer and the Christians in Tyre also understood the importance of involving their children in ministry. The jailer didn't have to bring Paul and Silas into his home for his family to hear the Gospel. He could have just talked to them in the prison and then passed along the message to his wife and kids later. Instead, he chose to involve his entire family. He reaped the benefit of this decision when everyone in his family gave their lives to the Lord.

A similar thing happened with the Christians in Tyre. Paul was preparing to leave these men and women to continue his missionary journey, and they gathered on the beach with their families to pray for him before he left. These Christians could have left their children at home. After all, they might have disturbed the prayer meeting or distracted the discussions. But instead, they chose to bring their kids along to pray with Paul and the other travelers because they didn't want their kids to miss the opportunity.

In our lives, we will have opportunities to serve and minister to those around us too. In these instances, it might be easier to leave our kids with a babysitter—less hassle, less preparation, and more progress. But, before we decide to hire a babysitter, we should ask ourselves what our kids might miss. When God is moving in the lives of His people, I don't want to stop my children from seeing it.

Questions for Reflection:

1. When have you involved your children in a ministry opportunity?

2. Sometimes it is better to leave your children at home instead of bringing them along in your ministry. Describe a time in which it would be unwise to involve your children.

3. What ministry are you involved in at church?

4. How could you include your children in this ministry?

Prayer:

God, I want my children to learn from my service. Help me to be creative as I think of ways to involve them in ministry. You have gifted them to serve. Please help me to get them involved in service. Amen.

Activities:

Day 1 – Adopt a missionary for your family to pray for on a weekly basis.

Day 2 – Enlist your child's help in some area of service this week.

Day 3 – In question three, I asked which ministry you are involved in at your local church. If you aren't involved in a ministry, call the church to see what ministries are available.

Day 4 – Talk with your church leadership about doing your own Great Day of Service in your community.

Day 5 – With your kids, give an hour to your local church and help with whatever the church needs done.

WEEK 52:
GOD THE FATHER

See what great love the Father has lavished on us, that we should be called children of God! And that is what we are! The reason the world does not know us is that it did not know him. 1 John 3:1

My husband is not the perfect parent, and neither am I, as I'm sure you can tell from reading many of the illustrations in this book. None of the biblical parents we've studied thus far are perfect either. Like us, they each made mistakes in their parenting. Some made huge mistakes that affected their children for the rest of their lives. But, there is one parent who is perfect and who never makes a mistake. He is our ultimate example.

We could talk about how He disciplines His children (see Hebrews 12:7). We could talk about how He challenges them to holiness and purity (see Matthew 5:48). We could talk about His mercy when His children mess everything up (see Romans 3:23; 6:23). But, there is one characteristic of our heavenly Father that stands out even more than these: His love.

I don't think I would be willing to sacrifice a child for a bunch of people who didn't like me. In fact, I don't think I'd be willing to sacrifice a child for those who did. Our Father, though, was willing. Even though we broke His heart with our sins, He still sent His Son to die for us. He loved us, His adopted children, that much.

Our kids might break our hearts. They might say they hate us or kick and scream when we try to help them. They might reject us in favor of their friends. It is in these instances we get the opportunity to love like our God does. Loving our kids is easy when they love us back, when they cuddle in our laps, or when they giggle as we tickle them. It's a lot more difficult when they spew words of hatred or disobey every rule in the home.

Parenting is difficult, plain and simple. Before I became a mom, I was convinced it would all come naturally. I thought I would have gushy feelings of love for my children all the time. I never expected it to be this hard. I never expected a day to come when I longed for bedtime or prayed for just a moment of alone time. I thought my days would be full of laughter and joy. At times, of course, they are. But at other times, being a mom is overwhelming and exhausting.

I think that's why God gave us the perfect example to follow. We can search the Internet, read parenting books, and explore magazines, but no other parent can claim perfection. No other parent but our Father. He will walk us through—day by day, year by year—He will be our guide. He might not give us a formula, but He will take us by the hand and lead us through the difficult days into greater wisdom. Our search began with confusion. It ends with perfection. Not our perfection, of course, but our Guide's.

Questions for Reflection:

1. Why does God love us so much, even when we seem unlovable?

2. Now that you have completed this devotional, how do you plan to continue searching the Scriptures for God's wisdom? In Appendix B, I've included 25 great Bible verses for you and your family to memorize. You could start there!

Prayer:

Father, thank you for loving me as your child. I am undeserving and unworthy, but you adopted me anyway. Help me to love my children as you have loved me: unconditionally. Guide me in the years to come as I raise my children into adults. Amen.

Activities:

Day 1 – List at least five ways in which God has loved you as His child.

Day 2 – List one specific way in which you can love your child as God has loved you.

Day 3 – Write each of your children a letter. Plan to give this letter to them when they are older.

Day 4 – Plan an entire day to celebrate each of your children.

Day 5 – You finished! Treat yourself to an ice cream or other dessert. ☺

To You, My Fellow Parents:

Congratulations! If you're reading this letter, that means one of two things. 1) You skipped ahead to the end of the book. Shame on you. Or, 2) You finished the entire devotional and should be proud of yourself! Like I said earlier, it's difficult to find time to go to the bathroom by yourself, let alone read an entire book. The fact that you finished shows just how much you care about your role as a parent. I hope you've gleaned some wisdom from the parents of the Bible through this book. (I know I did as I wrote it.)

Thanks for joining with me. It has been an honor to share this journey with you, and I would love to hear from you. If you want to connect with me further, you can find me online at any of these locations:

My website: www.lindseymbell.com

My blog: www.lindsey-bell.com
Twitter: www.twitter.com/LindseyMBell
Facebook: www.facebook.com/AuthorLindseyBell
Pinterest: www.pinterest.com/LindseyMBell01

Appendix A

Index of Topics:

Difficulties-Weeks 4, 6, 21, 22, 28, 30, 31, 34, 37, 39, 41, 43, 46, 47

Discipline-Weeks 18, 38

Leading by Example-Weeks 3, 11, 25, 26, 27, 36, 37, 42, 45, 50

Leaving a Legacy-Weeks 12, 13, 20, 27

Looking for Guidance-Weeks 1, 15, 19

Money- Weeks 24, 25, 35

Our Responsibility as Parents-Weeks 16, 17, 37, 39, 44, 48, 50

Prayer-Weeks 7, 23, 28, 31, 46

Priorities-Weeks 2, 5, 20, 29, 44, 46, 49

Remembering God's Blessings and Commands-Weeks 10, 33, 34

Representing God-Weeks 39, 48, 52

Index of Biblical Parents:

APPENDIX B – 25 KEY BIBLE VERSES:

Some of these verses are perfect as is, but others you might want to shorten for younger children. By the end of the year, if you memorize two a month, you'll have nearly all of them memorized.

On the Gospel Message:

Genesis 1:1 – *In the beginning God created the heavens and the earth.*

John 3:16 – *For God so loved the world that he gave his one and only Son, that whoever believes in him shall not perish but have eternal life.*

John 14:6 – *Jesus answered, "I am the way and the truth and the life. No one comes to the Father except through me."*

Romans 3:23 – *For all have sinned and fall short of the glory of God.*

On Our Actions:

Galatians 5:22-23 – *But the fruit of the Spirit is love, joy, peace, forbearance, kindness, goodness, faithfulness, gentleness and self-control. Against such things there is no law.*

Ephesians 4:32 – *Be kind and compassionate to one another, forgiving each other, just as in Christ God forgave you.*

Colossians 3:23 – *Whatever you do, work at it with all your heart, as working for the Lord, not for human masters.*

1 Timothy 4:12 – *Don't let anyone look down on you because you are young, but set an example for the believers in speech, in conduct, in love, in faith and in purity.*

On Our Anger:

James 1:19 – *My dear brothers and sisters, take note of this: Everyone should be quick to listen, slow to speak and slow to become angry.*

On Our Contentment:

Psalm 139:14 – *I praise you because I am fearfully and wonderfully made; your works are wonderful. I know that full well.*

Romans 8:28 – *And we know that in all things God works for the good of those who love him, who have been called according to his purpose.*

1 Thessalonians 5:16-18 – *Rejoice always; pray continually; give thanks in all circumstances; for this is God's will for you in Christ Jesus.*

On Our Love:

Deuteronomy 6:5 – *Love the LORD your God with all your heart and with all your soul and with all your strength.*

John 13:35 – *By this everyone will know that you are my disciples, if you love one another.*

1 Corinthians 13:4-7 – *Love is patient, love is kind. It does not envy, it does not boast, it is not proud. It does not dishonor others, it is not self-seeking, it is not easily angered, it keeps no record of wrongs. Love does not delight in evil but rejoices with the truth. It always protects, always trusts, always hopes, always perseveres.*

On Our Prayers:

Matthew 7:7 – *Ask and it will be given to you; seek and you will find; knock and the door will be opened to you.*

Colossians 4:2 – *Devote yourselves to prayer, being watchful and thankful.*

On Our Thoughts:

Philippians 4:8 – *Finally, brothers and sisters, whatever is true, whatever is noble, whatever is right, whatever is pure, whatever is lovely, whatever is admirable—if anything is excellent or praiseworthy—think about such things.*

Colossians 3:2 – *Set your minds on things above, not on earthly things.*

On Our Words:

Ephesians 4:29 – *Do not let any unwholesome talk come out of your mouths, but only what is helpful for building others up according to their needs, that it may benefit those who listen.*

On Our Worry/Fear:

Proverbs 18:10 – *The name of the LORD is a fortified tower; the righteous run to it and are safe.*

Matthew 11:28 – *Come to me, all you who are weary and burdened, and I will give you rest.*

Philippians 4:6 – *Do not be anxious about anything, but in every situation, by prayer and petition, with thanksgiving,* *present your requests to God.*

Philippians 4:13 – *I can do all this through him who gives me strength.*

1 Peter 5:7 – *Cast all your anxiety on him because he cares for you.*

Appendix C –
52 Money-Saving Tips:

Incorporate one tip a week and see how much money you save next year!

1. Start working on your budget. For the first three months, track your expenses —every single dime. In tip 12, I'll tell you what to do next.

2. Begin tithing to your local church if you aren't already.

3. Begin saving money every month (even if only a small amount).

4. Buy in bulk. Get a Sam's membership or watch for sales. When you see an item that's on sale, buy lots of it. The upfront expense is higher, but you save in the long run.

5. Buy generic. Most foods taste exactly the same. Test me on this. Do a blindfold taste test with a friend. Can you tell a difference between name brand and generic?

6. Create a list of 28-30 favorite meals. (This is preparation for Tip 7.)

7. Plan meals in advance. I recommend planning for a month at a time. You can rotate the meals you listed in Tip 6 for easy planning each month.

8. Make a shopping list every time you go to the store.

9. Only buy what's on your shopping list.

10. Never shop while hungry.

11. Start using the "envelope system," in which you budget money every month for expenses that regularly arise but aren't bills. (Some possible envelopes to include: birthdays, haircuts, entertainment, spending money, groceries, car insurance, etc.) If you're not familiar with the envelope system, send me an email, and I'll have more information

12. Create a budget spreadsheet from the information you've collected over the past three months. Include all expenses – regular bills, spending money, groceries, date money, envelopes from Tip 11, etc. Make sure your income exceeds your expenses.

13. Get an accountability partner to keep you on track with your budget.

14. Find things to reuse. For instance, use old shirts for rags, egg cartons for desk organizers, old magazines for homemade wrapping paper, leftover conditioner for shaving cream, etc. Be creative.

15. Start planning now for end-of-year expenses. Create an envelope for Christmas and for property taxes.

16. Plan for other unexpected expenses – new tires, car repairs, home repairs, etc.

17. Don't use coupons unless they actually save you money.

18. Find deal websites to check regularly.

19. Find free family activities. Google is your friend; use it.

20. Eat in more often than out.

21. Learn to say "no."

22. Cut out sweets and other unnecessary groceries.

23. Cut back on the amount of pop, coffee, and alcohol you drink.

24. Stop smoking or chewing tobacco.

25. Don't buy bottled water. It hurts the planet and your pocketbook.

26. Shop at garage sales and consignment stores.

27. Stop paying for childcare on date night. Instead, swap

date nights with another couple. You watch their kids while they go out and vice versa.

28. Re-evaluate your budget. Make changes as necessary.

29. Use average payment plans for electric and gas. It'll take the guesswork out of your bills. These companies readjust your bill at the end of the year to account for overpayment or underpayment.

30. Get books from the library, rather than buying them.

31. Add up all of your debt.

32. Pay off your credit card as fast as you can.

33. Get rid of most, if not all, of your credit cards. Use debit instead.

34. If you rarely use your home phone, get rid of the line.

35. Get rid of cable. I promise, it can be done.

36. Take your lunch to work instead of eating out.

37. Eat leftovers for several lunches a week.

38. Consider making your home more energy efficient.

39. Before making a large purchase, take at least a day (if not longer) to think it over.

40. Wait for sales to buy things. Consider waiting for the Black Friday sales.

41. Have a garage sale to make some extra money (or sell on Craigslist or eBay).

42. Cancel any unused memberships. I'm thinking gym …

43. Cut your own hair (or at least, cut the hair of all the males in the family).

44. Pack your own food for vacations or weekend trips.

45. Obey the speed limit. You won't have to worry about getting a ticket.

46. Eat less meat.

47. Draw names for Christmas instead of buying everyone a gift.

48. Make homemade gifts for Christmas. Again, use Google or Pinterest.

49. Look for extra sources of income.

50. When it's time for a new car, buy used. Cars lose most of their value in the first few years, so if you buy one that's a few years old, you get a much better deal.

51. Don't buy extended warranties.

52. Consider taking a Financial Peace University class. For more information, visit Dave Ramsey's website: www.daveramsey.com.

53. I know, this is Tip 53, but I had to include it. Don't give up! Keep at it, and you will eventually succeed. If you'd like some help and haven't downloaded *Financial Freedom on a Fixed Income* yet, please do it now by subscribing to my newsletters here: www.lindseymbell.com.

Endnotes

1. All Scripture quotations in this devotional are from the New International Version, unless otherwise noted.

2. I have changed some of the names of people within this devotional to protect the privacy of my friends and loved ones.

3. You are Not "Just a Mom" by Ruth Schwenk, blog post on July 17, 2013 http://www.momheart.org/2013/07/you-are-not-just-a-mom/

4. "A Son's First Hero, A Daughter's First Love" was written by Sonny Bell of Kansas City, MO and used with permission from Tess Bell.

Made in the USA
San Bernardino, CA
11 February 2019